THE FLOWER GARDEN

GROWING CUT FLOWERS ON YOUR WINDOWSILL

JENNITA JANSEN

ILLUSTRATIONS BY AGNES LOONSTRA

Hardie Grant

QUADRILLE

FOREWORD

So there I am, in my best shoes, standing among the weeds. A plot of land of about 100 square metres (330 square feet) on a thriving and lively community garden has just officially become mine. In good spirits, I start work in early spring, drawing on all kinds of knowledge that I gathered from books through the long winter evenings. I soon notice that I really enjoy growing flowers – bringing home bouquets that brighten up my living room, or quickly picking a beautiful posie before visiting family or friends. I also really love gardening, and that's how I came up with the idea for this book: everyone should know how much fun this is!

This book will help you to grow your own flowers. And even if you don't have a plot of land at your disposal, you can always grow flowers on a balcony or windowsill in boxes, pots or tubs. There are ideas for planting bulbs and tubers that will bloom in early spring, and we include some perennials for year-round colour. By following our planting schemes, or 'recipes', for the loveliest and easiest boxes full of flowers, you will soon have a balcony or windowsill that blooms and grows abundantly through the seasons. Not only will you find enjoyment in your new pastime, but you will also attract all kinds of insects, bees and butterflies to your beautiful blooms, helping to encourage biodiversity and making for greener living.

It is time get to work, I hope you really enjoy it!

Jennita Jansen

@plukatelier
Plukatelier.nl

CONTENTS

PART 1
THE BASICS

PRE-SOWING AND SOWING; WATERING, SUN, SHADE AND PARTIAL SHADE; WHERE DO YOU BEGIN? HERE YOU'LL FIND ALL THE INFORMATION YOU NEED FOR PREPARING AND MAINTAINING A SEA OF FLOWERS ON YOUR WINDOWSILL.

GARDENING IN BOXES

We use wooden boxes or crates for planting, but you can of course use pots or tubs. The handy thing with boxes is that they can simply stand on your balcony or windowsill. It is important that the boxes are deep enough – at least 40cm (16in) – so that the plants have room for strong roots to develop. To make optimum use of your outside space, if you have a balcony or roof terrace, you can make a stepped shelf with several boxes on top of each other. Place a box with a low-growing plant variety on the ground, and boxes with taller types on top. Make sure that you place the boxes on top of each other to form 'steps' so that they do not block the sunlight from those below.

GOOD SOIL

The soil is the growing medium for your flowers, so it must be of good quality. To begin, buy a couple of bags of organic potting compost (potting soil), which is an excellent base for germinating and growing your bloomers. With the nutrients in the soil, the plants can flourish for about 8 weeks. To extend the flowering time, you can sprinkle some extra organic compost in your boxes to top up the nutrients. Compost is organic material that is naturally generated from decomposted

plant residue. Some flowers in this book require some extra compost in the mid-growing and blooming season. For more information about these varieties, see pages 30–39.

TOOLS

For gardening in boxes, a few small gardening tools are all that is required. You can go a long way with a pair of gardening gloves, a small trowel, some sharp pruning shears and a watering can with a spray head. You can carefully pull out weeds by hand.

FLOWER GARDEN PESTS

You will notice that a lot of insects and animals are attracted to your flower garden, slugs and snails included, from which even your balcony isn't safe, because slugs can climb! That in itself can't do much harm, but it is a shame if they eat your germinated seedlings. As a natural deterrent, sprinkle some coffee grounds around your germinated plants; snails don't like the taste. They are not fans of broken eggshells either, as they can't crawl across them. Another option is to plant thyme between your flowers as snails hate the smell.

WATERING

In a sunny spot, the soil can dry out quickly. Check the soil; if it feels dry, give it some water. During a hot summer, you may need to do this twice a day. It is best to water early in the morning or late in the evening, giving lots of water in one go so that it can run deep into the soil. A long drink will soak into the base layer and stay in your box, rather than evaporating quickly from a lightly soaked top layer.

SUN

Most cut flowers love the sun and prefer to spend a considerable number of hours in sunlight. It is therefore important that there is sufficient daylight on your balcony or windowsill. You can find out how much sun and shade the different varieties need in the overview on pages 30–39. Discover how to map the sunny and shady spots on your balcony or windowsill on page 24. If you love a particular variety, just try it out, even if your balcony or windowsill is shaded more than the recommendation provided on the label.

SHIELDED FROM THE WIND

Plants do not like the wind, so give them a sheltered spot in which to grow.

AGASTACHE
RUGOSI

HELIANTHUS
ANNUUS

Achillea
filipendulina

DIGITALI

PRE-SOWING AND SOWING

SOWING IS NOT ROCKET SCIENCE; SIMPLY FOLLOW THE INSTRUCTIONS ON THE SEED PACKET. CERTAIN PLANTS CAN BE SOWN DIRECTLY IN THE GROUND FROM APRIL, OTHERS YOU REALLY HAVE TO PRE-SOW INDOORS AND THEY CAN ONLY BE PLANTED OUTSIDE AFTER THE RISK OF FROST HAS PASSED. PRE-SOWING WILL ACCELERATE THE FLOWERING SEASON.

As a general rule, seeds can usually cope well with frost, but young plants can't. Check the forecast from April to May; if the temperature stays above 10°C (50°F) during the day, you can sow the plants directly into your boxes. The best time is usually around mid-April. If it cools down considerably at night, protect the small plants against the cold or frost with a towel or bubble wrap. Make sure that the plants get enough light during the day to be able to grow.

INDOOR PROPAGATION

Pre-sow indoors from mid-February, so that you can accelerate the flowering of some plants. These pre-sown plants will flower earlier than the flowers you sow directly into your box. Use the step-by-step plan for pre-sowing on the following pages as a guide. Pre-sow in a propagator, egg carton or small pots, and place indoors in a sunny spot. The advantage of a propagator is that it has a lid to retain heat and moisture, so that the seeds can germinate well. Be careful not to overgrow your seedlings; tall-stemmed or 'leggy' plants are often not firm or strong enough to develop into healthy plants.

STEP-BY-STEP PRE-SOWING

WHAT YOU NEED

Containers for sowing (propagator, egg carton or pots), potting compost (soil), seeds, labels and a pen, spray water bottle

STEP 1

Fill your containers with potting compost to about 1cm (½in) below the edge and press lightly.

STEP 2

Divide the seeds between the containers, cover them with a thin layer of soil, and press gently. Some varieties are light germinators, which means that they don't need to be deep below the surface. Check the packet for the recommended sowing depth.

STEP 3

Write on the labels which varieties you have sown on which dates, and stick them in the corresponding spot in the soil.

STEP 4

Make sure the containers are placed in a bright, sunny spot.

STEP 5

Use the spray bottle on a light mist setting to water the soil so that the seeds stay in place. Do this every other day if the top soil fees dry to the touch. The soil should not become too dry, because then the germination process will stop, but not too wet either, as this will encourage mould growth.

STEP 6 PRICKING OUT

Germinating seeds will soon develop a few sprout leaves. After these sprout leaves you will see leaves appear that are different in shape; these are the real leaves. As soon as at least two of these leaves are visible, it is time to prick out the seedlings. That means transferring them to another, larger container so that the roots have more room to grow, but still leave them indoors. When pricking out, try not to damage the plants and their roots – they are still vulnerable at this stage. Carefully pry the seedlings out of the soil with the convex back of a teaspoon. Then lower the plant into the new container with soil in which you made a hole with your finger. Press the soil gently so that the plant stands firm and water immediately.

STEP 7 HARDENING OFF

Before you move the plants to their final location, they must first get used to the temperature outside. Putting them outside in a sheltered spot for a few days – and back inside at night – is a good way to prepare the plants. It is called 'hardening off' in gardener's jargon.

STEP 8 PLANTING

If you are certain there will be no more night frost, you can move the plants to their final location. To do this, loosen the soil a little and moisten it thoroughly; make holes in the soil, and place the plants about 15cm (6in) apart; press some soil around them. Give them some water and love and wait for those beautiful flowers.

EXTEND THE FLOWERING SEASON

If you only plant annual seedlings, then your flower garden will only blossom from May to October. Before and after this time there will be nothing to enjoy. To extend the growing and flowering season, you can also plant biennials, tubers and bulbs, and perennials. The following explains the difference.

ANNUALS

Annual flower varieties go through their natural life cycle from sprout to seed in one year. They flower in the same year they were sown. We sow these varieties in March, April or May, then they start to flower from June. After flowering, they produce seeds which spread themselves around the plant. With a little luck, they will flower again the following year. Sowing once does not necessarily mean that you will only enjoy the flowers once. After seed formation, the plant dies back.

BIENNIALS

Biennials first need a growing season to grow into flowering plants. The leaves often die in the autumn and winter, but the root survives underground and grows back into a plant in early spring. Then the flowers will often bloom early in the season because the plant has developed strong roots in the first year. In many cases biennials such as hollyhock and verbena live for a few more years after the first bloom, which is why they are also called perennials.

PERENNIALS

You sow or plant perennials once and they live forever. Well, forever might be a little too optimistic, but it is certain that they can withstand the winter cold well, so that they will shoot again the following year. Do water them now and then. Some remain green in winter; others die above ground but survive underground, and you will see them re-emerge the following year.

> **TIP**
> Plant a box with early spring bulbs such as daffodils and snowdrops. When they have finished flowering, leave them and sow annuals on top.

FLOWER BULBS

All nutrients are present in a flower bulb to allow the plant to bloom at the right time. Spring bloomers, such as daffodils and crocuses, need the frost to convert starch into sugar, which provides nutrients, so you plant them in the autumn. Summer bulbs, such as dahlias (see pages 82–85), begonias and anemones, should be dug up and stored in the winter. They bloom from summer to late autumn (see also page 16).

SOW OR BUY PLANTS?

In this book, we assume that you will sow the plants yourself and also pre-sow, but you can also buy plants from a garden centre or nursery, which will give you an instant effect and guaranteed success. Plants are easy to combine with the varieties that you sow yourself. When buying fully grown plants, check with the seller that the plants are not sprayed with pesticide. Sprayed flowers are disastrous for bees and butterflies and are one of the causes of the decline of these insects.

COLD GERMINATORS

Many types of flowers need a cold period. This means that they only become active once they have suffered the cold for a few weeks. You therefore sow these varieties outside in the autumn and/or winter, between October and February, when the temperatures are still low. Then you just let nature do its job. In the spring, the seeds germinate when they are ready. Flowering usually follows in the same spring and/or summer.

+ **Love-in-a-mist:** sow in October (1)
+ **Great masterwort:** sow in October and November (2)
+ **Verbena:** sow in September and October (3)
+ **Cornflower:** sow in October and November (4)
+ **Monkshood:** sow in October (5)
+ **Ox-eye daisy:** sow in September and October
+ **Quaking grass:** sow in September and October
+ **Switchgrass:** sow in September and October

PLANTING FLOWER BULBS

To be able to enjoy spring colour long before the 'normal' flowering season, you can plant bulbs in the autumn. Do you want snowdrops in December and January? Then plant the bulbs in September. Plant real heralders of spring, such as daffodils, from October to November, then they will flower from February to April/May, depending on the variety you choose.

OPTIMIZING SPACE

To make optimal use of your container, you can plant the bulbs in layers, building different layers with flower bulbs that flower shortly after each other, or overlap each other slightly in terms of flowering time. Plant the variety that flowers last at the bottom of the container, on top of that comes the variety that flowers second and at the top of your container the variety that flowers earliest. Do not place the bulbs too close together in the soil, to allow enough room for the underlying bulb to grow in between.

REUSE YOUR BULBS

Spring bulbs such as snake's head, grape hyacinth, snowdrops, daffodils, lily-of-the-valley and allium 'Mohican' can be left in your container all year round. They sprout year after year. An exception to this are tulips. These are also spring bulbs, but they flower less well in the second year. After flowering, place the tulips in a sheltered, light spot (if they were not already there), cut out the dead flowers and let the leaves die off slowly. Water occasionally to keep the bulbs from drying out. Once all the leaves and stems have died, remove the bulbs from the ground, which is called 'grubbing up'. Wipe them clean to remove soil and store them in a cardboard box. Place newspaper between the layers of bulbs and store the box in a dry, cool place. In the autumn, they can go back into the ground.

TIP
Have you been given a pot with a spring bloomer as a gift? After flowering, do not throw away the bulbs; put them in your box.

SPRING BULBS IN LAYERS

TIPS FOR PLANTING BULBS

+ Plant the bulb right way up with the tip pointing upwards
+ The bulbs should not touch each other
+ The layer of soil between the different bulb varieties must be at least 5cm (2in) deep
+ Firm the soil well during planting
+ The best time to plant your spring bulbs is late October to November. Summer bulbs such as the dahlia, should be planted in March/April to start flowering in the summer.

The container in which you plant three layers must be at least 35cm (14in) deep.

5-7CM
(2-2³/₄IN)

CARING FOR YOUR PLANTS

ONCE YOUR SEEDS HAVE SPROUTED, THEY NEED PROPER CARE SO THAT THEY CAN GROW INTO LARGE, STRONG PLANTS. YOU'LL NEED TO SUPPORT, FERTILIZE, WEED AND HARVEST SEEDS. HOW EXACTLY DO YOU DO THAT? FIND OUT ALL YOU NEED FOR FLOWERING SUCCESS IN THIS SECTION.

SUPPORT CANES

Tall flower varieties such as cosmos and dahlia can droop a bit, or grow crookedly. To give them some support, tie the plants to bamboo canes using flexible twine. Do not pull the twine too tight, as the stem will also get thicker, and a squeezed stalk can no longer absorb moisture from the soil.

FERTILIZING

Many of your plants can use extra nutrition midway through their flowering season, in late July or early August, for example. Use organic, in other words natural, fertilizer for this. It is broken down in the soil, then the plants absorb the nutrient-rich minerals. Part of this organic matter remains in the soil, which improves the overall quality in the long term.

DEAD HEADING

Many flowers put their energy into making seeds after flowering, instead of making new flower buds. If you keep removing the dead flowers, known as dead heading, the plant can't produce any seeds and you can enjoy more flowers for much longer.

WEED CONTROL

When growing flowers in containers, the amount of weeds between your flowers is probably fairly minimal, but it is still worth keeping an eye on any possible overgrowth. Weeds also benefit from the nutrients contained in the soil, while of course you prefer to see the nutrients go to your flowers. You can easily remove weeds by simply pulling them out by hand.

HARVESTING YOUR OWN SEEDS

When annual varieties have finished flowering, they will start making seeds. Seeds are by no means always tiny black dots. For example, they can also look like caterpillars or feathers. They lie in the core of the flower, or are in seed pods that form after flowering. This creates a kind of drum in which the seeds ripen and dry. As soon as the seeds are well dried, the drum bursts open and the seeds fall to the ground. This means that the plant self-seeds and the variety remains represented in nature.

If you want to harvest your own seeds, let the flowers bloom and wither, then you will automatically see where the seeds form. How you should harvest depends on how a plant produces seeds (see page 22).

PREPARING BOXES FOR WINTER

In late October and early November, it is time to prepare your boxes for winter. Remove any remaining or dying annual plants carefully from the box. Spring bulbs (except tulips, see page 16) can be left in the box. You can leave perennials in the box after flowering; the foliage will slowly die back. In March, cut the plants back all the way to, or close to, the base of the stem. In this way, it will shoot again and start flowering in the summer.

FLOWERING SEASONS

The exact time when plants flower can vary by several weeks, depending on your local climate. For general reference though, horticulturalists define the flowering seasons in the Northern Hemisphere as:

SPRING: March, April, May
SUMMER: June, July, August
AUTUMN: September, October, November
WINTER: December, January, February

STEP-BY-STEP HARVESTING SEEDS

STEP 1 PREPARATION

Leave a few flowers of the varieties from which you want to harvest seeds and allow to go to seed. For this purpose, choose a plant that looks strong and healthy. After flowering, you can see the flower wither, then the seeds are formed.

STEP 2 RECOGNIZING SEEDS

There are countless different types of seeds, sometimes as tiny as grains of sand, but there are also bean-shaped ones or those that resemble small feathers. You will see them appear where the heart of the flower used to be. In some varieties, such as the poppy, you will see a small drum containing the seeds.

STEP 3 HARVESTING

Once the seeds are ripe and dry, they can be harvested. Plants make seeds in different ways, which is why harvesting is not the same for all varieties. For example:

+ Lupins and hollyhocks form seed pods that dry slowly. Once they are completely dried, you can start harvesting the seeds. Often the pods at the bottom of the stems are 'ripe' sooner. Then leave the top ones for a while to dry further.

+ With many varieties such as cosmos, cornflower, poppy and pot marigold, you can cut off the entire flower stem without any seeds falling off. Tap the stems over a bucket or pot that will catch the seeds as soon as they fall off the stem. You can also tie a paper bag around the seed pods and hang the plant upside down to dry further. The seeds will then automatically fall into the bag.

STEP 4 DRYING

After harvesting the seeds it is important to allow them to dry. In this way, their germination rate will be maintained and you can sow them again successfully the following year. Spread the seeds on newspaper and place them in an open container or on a tray. Immediately write down which variety you are drying and place the seeds in a dry, not too warm place indoors, away from the sun. Let the seeds dry from a few days up to a week.

STEP 5 CLEANING

Clean the dried seed as well as possible. Sift the seed (for example through a tea strainer) to remove the seed pods and small plant debris. You can also simply blow very fine seeds: lay the seed on your hand and gently blow over it. Because the seed is heavier than the chaff, you will blow that away and the seeds will remain.

STEP 6 STORAGE

As soon as the seeds are nice and clean, put them in a paper bag or envelope clearly labelled with the name of the variety. It is important not to use plastic bags for this, as the seed can 'sweat' and lose its germinative power. Then keep the full seed bags in a dry, dark and cool place.

It is very easy to harvest seeds from the following varieties used in this book: cosmos, pot marigold, love-in-a-mist, sweet pea, poppy and sunflower.

WORKING WITH THE SUN

IT'S TIME TO CHOOSE THE FLOWERS FOR YOUR CUT FLOWER GARDEN. TO HELP DECIDE WHICH FLOWERS WILL THRIVE IN YOUR SPOT, YOU NEED TO MAP THE HOURS OF SUNSHINE ON YOUR BALCONY OR WINDOWSILL. THEN YOU CAN MATCH VARIETIES SUITED TO SUN, PARTIAL SHADE OR SHADE.

It is useful to make a garden calendar so that you know what flowers to plant, when they will bloom and in which month you have to start sowing or pre-sowing. You can also see which boxes you can reuse after summer flowering, for example, by planting spring bulbs in the autumn to enjoy flowers early next year.

PLAN AHEAD

Step 1: Map the hours of sunshine
Step 2: Choose your flowers and buy the seeds and all the supplies
Step 3: Prepare your boxes, sow, care for and then... enjoy your sea of flowers, both outside and inside

SUN, PARTIAL SHADE OR SHADE

Which flowers will do well in your outdoor space depends on how much sun they get per day. Keep track of the sun hours to find out what flowers best suit your outside space.

TALLYING HOURS OF SUNSHINE

Observe when the sun appears and when the spot falls into the shade again. Add up the hours and, hey presto, now you know which flowers are best for your balcony or windowsill. For example, if the sun appears at 11am and is gone at 5pm, then you have 6 hours of sunshine. And that is enough sun for flowers that love sunshine.

Some plants thrive in both sun and partial shade. The preferred planting positions will be listed on the seed packet with the following symbols: ☀ and ☀. The position can have a significant affect on flowering. In the sun, such a plant will produce many flowers, while it will flower less abundantly in the shade. The same goes for plants that like partial shade/shade. They usually bloom more beautifully in partial shade. These plants usually do not survive in full sun.

POSITION

- ☀ **Position in full sun:** at least 5–6 hours of sun per day.
- ☀ **Position in partial shade:** maximum 5 and minimum 3 hours of sun per day.
- ☀ **Position in shade:** maximum 2 hours of full sun per day. Shade plants can also be placed in the darker areas of your balcony or windowsill. If there is no sun at all on the balcony or windowsill, it is better to accept that the varieties you choose will not flower as profusely.

WHAT PLANT WHERE?

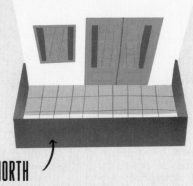

EAST

East-facing balcony or windowsill: morning sun. Mainly shade by midday. Opt for partial shade plants (see pages 34–37).

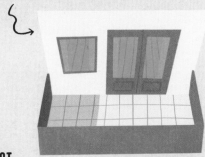

NORTH

North-facing balcony or windowsill: plenty of shade, no direct sunlight. Unfortunately, there are no cut flower varieties that thrive in complete shade. Try out some partial shade plants (see pages 38–39) and see how they do.

WEST

West-facing balcony or windowsill: plenty of shade in the morning and plenty of sun in the afternoon and evening. Opt for partial shade plants and sun worshippers (see pages 30–34).

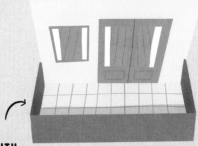

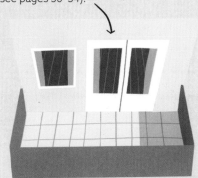

SOUTH

South-facing balcony or windowsill: plenty of sun, choose sun worshippers (see pages 30–34). *Note:* water twice a day when the sun is shining brightly.

Zonnebloem
Lathyrus
Kievitsbloem
Strobloem
kap
Duizendblad
Zinnia
Zeeuws Knoopje
Dahlia
Korenbloem
lelietje van Dalen
Zonnehoed

SUN AND SHADE FLOWERS

ON THE FOLLOWING PAGES YOU WILL FIND OUR FAVOURITE CUTTING FLOWERS FOR YOUR BALCONY OR WINDOWSILL, SORTED BY THE NUMBER OF HOURS OF SUNSHINE THEY CAN TOLERATE AND IN ORDER OF FLOWERING TIME.

We have chosen to list the common names of the plants first, because they are often easier to remember than the Latin variants. But, if you order seeds or plants from a nursery, it is important to also know the scientific Latin name, because in many cases several varieties will fall under one common name. The Latin names are more extensive and therefore more precise, listing both genus and species, and sometimes a cultivar, such as *Astrantia major* 'Albus'. They are used as standard by suppliers throughout the world.

SUN-LOVING FLOWERS

MOST CUTTING FLOWERS LOVE THE FULL SUN. SUN WORSHIPPERS PREFER TO BE AT LEAST 6 HOURS A DAY IN THE SUN AND USE ALL THE SUN'S RAYS THAT THEY CAN GET TO PRODUCE AS MANY FLOWERS AS POSSIBLE. THE HEAT CAUSES THE SOIL TO DRY OUT QUICKLY, SO MAKE SURE YOU WATER THEM WELL.

AQUILEGIA

Aquilegia vulgaris
Pre-sow indoors: March–April
Sow direct: April–May

Position: ☀ / ☀
Height: 80cm (31½in)
Flowering time: April–July
Dried flowers: no
Perennial, when sown will flower in the second year

POPPY

Papaver somniferum
Pre-sow indoors: no
Sow direct: March–May

Position: ☀
Height: 40-60cm (16-24in)
Flowering time: May–July
Dried flowers: yes, seed pods
Annual

ECHINACEA

Echinacea
Pre-sow indoors: March–April
Sow direct: May–July

Position: ☀
Height: 100cm (40in)
Flowering time: July–Oct
Dried flowers: no
Perennial, when sown will flower in the second year

OX-EYE DAISY

Leucanthemum vulgare
Pre-sow indoors: no
Sow direct: April–May and Sept–Oct

Position: ☀
Height: 50–60cm (20–24in)
Flowering time: May–Sept
Dried flowers: no
Perennial

POT MAIGOLD

Calendula officinalis
Pre-sow indoors: no
Sow direct: from mid-April–June

Position: ☀
Height: 30–50cm (12–20in)
Flowering time: May–Oct
Dried flowers: no
Annual

LOVE-IN-A-MIST

Nigella damascena
Pre-sow indoors: no
Sow direct: from March–June

Position: ☀
Height: 30–60cm (12–24in)
Flowering time: June–Aug
Dried flowers: yes, seed heads
Annual

BISHOP'S FLOWER

Ammi majus
Pre-sow indoors: no
Sow direct: from mid-Feb–May

Position: ☀
Height: 50–100cm (20–40in)
Flowering time: June–Sept
Dried flowers: no
Annual

YARROW

*Achilla filipendulina
'Cloth of Gold'*
Pre-sow indoors: March–April
or July–Sept
Sow direct: late April–May
or July–Sept

Position: ☀ / ☀
Height: 80–120cm (31½–47in)
Flowering time: June–Sept
Dried flowers: yes
*Perennial, when sown will
flower in the second year*

DAHLA

Dahlia
Indoors before planting:
from mid-March in a pot in
a sunny spot
Plant tubers: mid-May

Position: ☀
Height: 30–150cm (12–60in)
Flowering time: mid-July
to the first night frost
Dried flowers: no
Annual – tubers are perennial

SMALL SCABIOUS

Scabiosa atropurpurea
Pre-sow indoors: from
mid-March
Sow direct: April–June

Position: ☀ / ☀
Height: 50–75cm (20–29½in)
Flowering time: July–Sept
Dried flowers: no
Annual

GLOBE THISTLE

Echinops
Pre-sow indoors: no
Sow direct: mid-May–June

Position: ☀
Height: 100cm (40in)
Flowering time: July–Sept
Dried flowers: yes
*Perennial, when sown will
flower in the second year*

CORNFLOWER

Centaurea cyanus
Pre-sow indoors: no
Sow direct: late March–May
and Oct–Nov

Position: ☀ / ☀
Height: 40–60cm (16–24in)
Flowering time: June–Sept
Dried flowers: yes
Annual

SWEET PEA

Lathyrus odoratus
Pre-sow indoors:
from mid Feb
Sow direct: from mid-
April–late May

Position: ☀
Height: 180cm (71in)
Flowering time: June–Sept
Dried flowers: no
Annual

WINGED EVERLASTING IMMORTELLE

Xeranthemum annuum
Pre-sow indoors: March–April
Sow direct: April–May

Position ◐ / ☀
Height: 40–90cm (16–35in)
Flowering time: June–Sept
Dried flowers: yes
Annual

SUNFLOWER

Helianthus annuus
'Pacino'
Pre-sow indoors: March–April
Sow direct: April–May

Position ◐
Height: 45–60cm (18–24in)
Flowering time: July–Sept
Dried flowers: no
Annual

ZINNIA

Zinnia elegans
'California Giants'
Pre-sow indoors: late
March–early April
Sow direct: mid May–June

Position ☀
Height: 30–70cm (12–28in)
Flowering time: July–Oct
Dried flowers: no
Annual

COSMOS

Cosmos bipinnatus
Pre-sow indoors: April
Sow direct: May–June

Position ◐
Height: 80cm (31½in)
Flowering time: July–Oct
Dried flowers: no
Annual

BUPLEURUM

Bupleurum rotundifolium
'Griffithii'
Pre-sow indoors: March–April
Sow direct: April–May

Position ◐
Height: 60cm (24in)
Flowering time: July–Oct
Dried flowers: no
Annual

SUN AND PARTIAL SHADE FLOWERS

PLANTS OR SEEDS WITH THE FOLLOWING SYMBOLS ON THE LABEL ☀ / ☀ CAN WITHSTAND SUN AND PARTIAL SHADE, AND WILL FLOWER A LITTLE MORE IN THE SUN THAN IN PARTIAL SHADE. ALWAYS KEEP A CLOSE EYE ON THE FLOWERS, WHEN PARTIAL SHADE FLOWERS ARE IN THE SUN, YOU MUST ENSURE THAT THE OTHER CONDITIONS ARE GOOD. SO GIVE ENOUGH WATER AND PUT THE PLANTS IN A SHELTERED PLACE.

SNOWDROP

Galanthus nivalis
Plant bulbs: Sept–Dec

Position ☼ / ☀
Height: 15cm (6in)
Flowering time: Jan–March
Dried flowers: no

DAFFODIL

Narcissus bulbocodium
'Golden Bells'
Plant bulbs: Sept–Dec

Position ☼ / ☀
Height: 15cm (6in)
Flowering time: March–May
Dried flowers: no

SNAKE'S HEAD

Fritillaria meleagris
Plant bulbs: Aug–Dec

Position ☼ / ☀
Height: 30cm (12in)
Flowering time: April–May
Dried flowers: no

TULIP

Tulipa 'Black Parrot'
Plant bulbs: Sept–Dec

Position ☼ / ☀
Height: 60cm (24in)
Flowering time: April–June
Dried flowers: no

LILY-OF-THE-VALLEY

Convallaria majalis
Plant bulbs: Sept–Nov

Position ☼ / ☀
Height: 25cm (10in)
Flowering time: May–June
Dried flowers: no

QUAKING GRASS

Briza media
Plant bulbs: April–June or
Sept–Oct

Position ☼ / ☀
Height: 50–60cm (20–24in)
Flowering time: May–Aug
Dried flowers: yes
Perennial

LUPIN

Lupinus luteus
Plant bulbs: March–April

Position ☀ / ☀
Height: 80cm (31½in)
Flowering time: May–Aug
Dried flowers: no
Annual

GYSOPHILA

Gysophila elegans
Pre-sow indoors: no
Sow direct: May–June

Position ☀ / ☀
Height: 50cm (20in)
Flowering time: June–Sep
Dried flowers: yes
Annual

GREAT MASTERWORT

Astrantia major 'Alba'
Sow direct: Oct-Nov

Position ☀ / ☀
Height: 60cm (24in)
Flowering time: June–Sept
Dried flowers: yes
Perennial

VERBENA

Verbena bonariensis
Sow direct: Feb–April or
Sept–Oct

Position ☀ / ☀
Height: 150cm (60in)
Flowering time: June–Oct
Dried flowers: no
Biennial

STRAWFLOWER

Helichrysum bracteatum
Pre-sow inoors: no
Sow direct: April–May

Position ☀ / ☀
Height: 50–80cm (20–31½in)
Flowering time: June–Oct
Dried flowers: yes
Annual

ALLIUM

Allium
'Red Mohican'
Plant bulbs: Aug–Dec

Position ☀ / ☀
Height: 100cm (40in)
Flowering time: July–Aug
Dried flowers: no

AUTUMN ASTER

Aster novae-angliae
Plant: autumn or spring
(before flowering)

Position ☽ / ☀
Height: 120cm (47in)
Flowering time: Sept–Oct
Dried flowers: yes
Perennial

SEED AND BULB SUPPLIERS

famflowerfarm.com

UNITED KINGDOM
sarahraven.com
chilternseeds.co.uk
higgledygarden.com
swancottageflowers.co.uk
vitalseeds.co.uk

UNITED STATES
johnnyseeds.com
floretflowers.com
berbeeus.com
swallowtailgardenseeds.com

TIME AWAY

If you are away from home for a few days, try this trick with a plastic bottle to prevent your plants drying out. Using scissors, make a hole in the cap of a full bottle of water. Invert the bottle so the neck is in your box. The water will run slowly through the hole in the cap into the soil and your plants won't be thirsty.

PARTIAL SHADE AND SHADE FLOWERS

IDEALLY, THESE TYPES OF FLOWERS HAVE MORNING OR EVENING SUN SO THAT THEY ARE IN THE SHADE AT THE HOTTEST TIME OF THE DAY. ALSO, MAKE SURE THAT FOR PARTIAL SHADE PLANTS, THE SOIL IS KEPT MOIST.

PERENNIAL HONESTY

Lunaria rediviva
Pre-sow indoors: Feb–March
Sow direct: June–July

Position: ☀ / ☀
Height: 100cm (40in)
Flowering time: April–June
Dried flowers: yes, seed pods
*Perennial, when sown will
flower in the second year*

FOXGLOVE

Digitalis purpurea
Sow direct: June–Aug
Plant: Oct–Nov

Position: ☀
Height: 80–150cm (31½–60in)
Flowering time: April–Oct
Dried flowers: no
Biennial

MONKSHOOD

Aconitum napellus
Sow direct: Oct

Position: ☀
Height: 150cm (60in)
Flowering time: June–Oct
Dried flowers: no
*Perennial, when sown will
flower in the second year*

AGASTACHE

Agastache rugosa
'Golden Jubilee'
Plant: March or late summer

Position: ☀ / ☀
Height: 50–70cm (20–28in)
Flowering time: July–Sept
Dried flowers: no
Perennial

SWITCHGRASS

Panicum vigratum
Pre-sow indoors: under glass
in mid-March to early April
Plant: after mid-May

Position: ☀
Height: 120–150cm (47–60in)
Flowering time: July–Aug
Dried flowers: yes
Perennial

JAPANESE ANEMONE

Anemone hupehensis
Plant: autum or spring
(before floweing)

Position: ☀
Height: 70cm (28in)
Flowering time: Sept–Oct
Dried flowers: yes, seed
heads *Perennial*

PREPARING THE BOXES

**TIME TO GET CRACKING. BEFORE YOU START
SOWING, FIRST PREPARE YOUR BOXES.**

Which boxes you choose for your cut flower garden is of course up to you. However, there are a few things to take into account. If you use wooden boxes, make sure that they are at least 40cm (16in) deep, and measure 50 x 60cm (20 x 24in). You can sow about three varieties of seeds/plants in one box. If you use fruit crates, there will likely be large openings between the slats. If you fill a fruit crate with soil, everything will fall out at the bottom, and of course you don't want that! To help, line the box with water-permeable anti-root cloth. This black polyester fabric, which allows water to pass through, is available at garden centres and home improvement stores.

You can also use plastic grout tubs with a diameter of at least 50cm (20in). For good drainage, make some holes in the bottom and side using a drill. This is also recommended for large stone pots that are solid at the bottom.

BOX BASICS
What you need
+ Boxes, tubs or large pots
+ For boxes only: anti-root cloth
+ A few bags of potting compost (soil)
+ Hydro grains

STEP-BY-STEP PREPARATION

STEP 1

Choose a suitable spot in your garden, or on your balcony or windowsill where you want to place the boxes.

STEP 2

Place the anti-root cloth over the box and push it down so that it covers the bottom and sides. Cut it to the correct size; it won't look attractive if the flaps are hanging over the edge. Anti-root cloth is not necessary for a closed plastic tub or stone pot.

STEP 3

Sprinkle a layer of about 5cm (2in) of hydro grains in the box. These are small balls of clay that absorb water and release a little each time, so that the soil remains moist. Then throw potting compost over the hydro grains up to about 20cm (8in) below the edge of the box. Level the soil with a trowel for a perfectly smooth seed bed.

STEP 4

Your boxes are now ready for sowing! See the following chapters for ideas and instructions on how to sow your boxes.

PART 2

PLANTING SCHEMES

YOUR BOX IS PREPARED AND YOU KNOW WHETHER TO GROW PLANTS FOR SUN OR PARTIAL SHADE – NOW IT'S TIME TO CHOOSE FLOWERS, BUY SEEDS AND JUST SOW! HERE WE SUGGEST COLOURFUL AND SEASONALCOMBINATIONS, BUT OF COURSE YOU CAN MAKE YOUR BOXES AS BEAUTIFUL AND VARIED AS YOU LIKE. WE ASSUME THAT YOU WILL SOW DIRECT IN THE BOX BUT WHERE IT IS MORE CONVENIENT TO PRE-SOW, SO THAT ALL THE FLOWERS BLOOM AT THE SAME TIME, YOU WILL FIND DETAILS ON HOW TO PLAN AHEAD.

BOXES FOR SUN

CUT FLOWERS ARE SUN WORSHIPPERS. THE BOXES ON THE FOLLOWING PAGES CAN THEREFORE ALL BE POSITIONED IN FULL SUN, AS LONG AS YOU PROVIDE SUFFICIENT WATER.

SUPER SEASONAL BLOOMERS

A BOX FULL OF FLOWERS IN VARIOUS COLOURS AND SHAPES: ZINNIAS PROVIDE AN EXPLOSION OF COLOUR MIXED WITH THE SUBTLE LACE OF BISHOP'S FLOWERS AND GRACEFUL LOVE-IN-A-MIST. THE PLANTS IN THIS BOX ALL FLOWER ABUNDANTLY, FROM APRIL TO LATE SUMMER.

☀ **Position:** sun

❋ **Sow:** sow all varieties at the same time, in April. The bishop's flower and love-in-the-mist can also be sown earlier in March and April

❋ **Flowering time:** April–August

1. Zinnia **2.** Love-in-a-mist **3.** Bishop's Flower

TIP

Take care with young plants and snails. In one night, snails can eat away all your seedlings back to the soil.

GETTING STARTED

1. Fill the box to about 20cm (8in) below the edge with potting compost.

2. Sow the bishop's flower about 2cm (¾in) deep in the back of the box, as these will grow the tallest.

3. Leave a space of 15cm (6in) from the bishop's flower and sow the zinnia seeds.

4. Leave another space of 15cm (6in) and sow the love-in-a-mist at the front.

5. Cover the seeds with a thin layer of soil and carefully press level.

6. Mist with water from a spray bottle, so that the seeds stay in place.

7. If necessary, stick plant labels in the soil, stating which varieties you have sown in this box.

WHAT YOU NEED

- READY-TO-USE BOX *(40cm/16in deep)* *with 5cm (2in) hydro grains and 5cm (2in) potting compost (soil)*
- EXTRA POTTING COMPOST (SOIL)
- BAG OF HYDRO GRAINS
- ZINNIA SEEDS *(Zinnia elegans* 'California Giants'*)*
- BISHOP'S FLOWER SEEDS *(Ammi majus)*
- LOVE-IN-A-MIST SEEDS *(Nigella damascena)*

FLOWERS

+ ZINNIA
(Zinnia elegans 'California Giants'*)*

This zinnia variety has well-filled, colourful flowers, which are very popular with butterflies. The seed mix contains yellow, pink, orange and red flowers. Zinnias flower until autumn and are therefore perfect for cut flower boxes to provide posies all summer long. To test if your zinnias are ready to pick, hold the stem about 8cm (3in) below the flower and gently shake it back and forth. If the stem stays firm and straight, the time has come!

+ BISHOP'S FLOWER *(Ammi majus)*

The white umbels stand on fragile stems and are surrounded by dill-like fresh green foliage. The flowers can be kept in a vase for up to 10 days and are very suitable for filling in bouquets. When it has finished flowering, the bishop's flower is lovely and very useful in dried bouquets.

+ LOVE-IN-A-MIST *(Nigella damascena)*

This flower has something exotic about it, with its slender leaves, and bees are very attracted to it. After flowering, the flower forms the most beautiful seed pods that you can use in dried bouquets.

CARE

Dead head your plants to stimulate the production of new flowers. These varieties are annual, so after flowering you can let them die back then remove them.

TIP

Home-grown zinnias are edible. That is, if you don't use pesticides. The petals add colour to salads and soups, and look festive in carafes of water. The leaves have a light, spicy taste.

HERALDERS OF SPRING

BUPLEURUM, OX-EYE DAISY AND POT MARIGOLD ARE THREE HARDY PLANTS THAT YOU CAN SOW DIRECT IN YOUR BOX FROM APRIL. CUT THE DEAD FLOWERS AWAY AND THE PLANTS WILL PRODUCE NEW BUDS LIKE CRAZY.

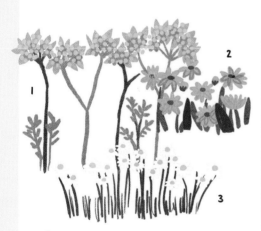

☀ **Position:** sun

❀ **Sow:** all varieties can be sown directly in the ground from mid April

✿ **Flowering time:** May–October

1. Bupleurum **2.** Pot Marigold
3. Ox-Eye Daisy

WHAT YOU NEED

+ A READY-TO-USE BOX *(40cm/16in deep) with 5cm (2in) of hydro grains and 5cm (2in) potting compost (soil)*
+ EXTRA POTTING COMPOST (SOIL)
+ BUPLEURUM SEEDS *(Bupleurum rotundifolium 'Griffithii')*
+ POT MARIGOLD SEEDS *(Calendula officinalis)*
+ OX-EYE DAISY SEEDS *(Leucanthemum vulgare)*

FLOWERS

◆ BUPLEURUM
(Bupleurum rotundifolium 'Griffithii')
Germinates within 3 weeks after sowing.
Is night frost still forecast? Then cover the
seedlings with an upside-down flower pot
or plastic sheet to protect them from the
worst cold. It is also an easy plant with
beautiful flowers that are surrounded by
sturdy blue-green foliage. Pick them
as soon as the flowers are fully open.
They last well in a vase for up to 10 days
and are also suitable for use in dried
flower bouquets.

◆ OX-EYE DAISY *(Leucanthemum vulgare)*
Can be sown during two periods of the
year; between mid-April and mid-May for
flowering in the same year, and September
and October for flowering in the following
early spring. The flowers will bloom about
12 weeks after you have sown them. The
ox-eye daisy does not require much care,
but it is not drought resistant.

◆ POT MARIGOLD *(Calendula officinalis)*
Sow directly in the ground from mid-April.
An easy variety that germinates within a
few weeks. You can sow the pot marigold
again in May and/or June to prolong the
flowering and these seeds will flower that
same year! Pot marigolds self-seed easily
and can even survive mild winters. In a

FLOWER FACT
The ox-eye daisy is edible and
makes a nice addition to salads.
You can pickle the flower buds
in vinegar for using as capers.

vase they remain beautiful for about
6 days, which isn't very long but, because
they bloom so profusely, you can pick
fresh flowers often. The leaves of the
pot marigold are a bit sticky. To protect
your hands, wear gardening gloves
when cutting the flowers.

**All flowers will produce more buds
if you cut out the dead flowers.**

CARE

This box is full of strong varieties, but
they do need a lot of moisture, especially
in the beginning when they are starting to
germinate. Check your box every day
during this phase to see if the soil is still
a bit wet. If the seedlings grow too close
together, thin them out a little. If you cut
the ox-eye daisy back to about 15cm (6in)
above the ground after the first bloom,
you have a chance that flowers will appear
again in late summer.

I

↕ 20CM (8IN)

GETTING STARTED

1. Fill the prepared box to about 20cm (8in) below the edge with potting compost.

2. Sow the bupleurum in the back of your box, as these will grow the tallest.

3. Leave a space of 15cm (6in) from the bupleurum and sow the ox-eye daisy seeds.

4. Leave another space of 15cm (6in) and sow the pot marigolds in the front.

5. Cover the seeds with a thin layer of soil and carefully press it level.

6. Mist with water from a spray bottle so that the seeds remain in place.

You can also mix the seeds of these varieties. Make sure you remove some seedlings as soon as they sprout; the plants need some space to grow. Keep a minimum distance of about 15cm (6in) between the seedlings.

3

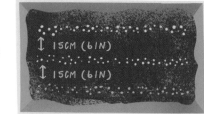

↕ 15CM (6IN)
↕ 15CM (6IN)

SUN LOVERS

**THE CORNFLOWER, LUPIN AND POPPY IN THIS BOX
ALL LOVE THE FULL SUN. THE FIRST BUDS WILL OPEN FROM
LATE JUNE AND THE BOX WILL BE FILLED WITH FLOWERS,
WHICH WILL BLOOM WELL INTO SEPTEMBER.**

☀ **Position:** sun

❀ **Sow:** you can pre-sow lupin indoors in late February/March and plant the plants in your box from mid-May, where the cornflower and poppy seedlings have already sprouted. If it freezes again, cover the box with a towel at night. For the lupin, this can be done a month later, in mid-April. If you just want to sow all the varieties directly in the soil, do this from mid-April. Then they will flower one after the other.

✿ **Flowering time:** June–September

1. Lupin **2.** Cornflower **3.** Poppy

GETTING STARTED

1. Fill the prepared box to about 15cm (6in) below the edge with potting compost.
2. Sow the lupin seeds about 2cm (5in) deep at the back of your box, as these will grow the highest. Or, if you are pre-sowing the lupin indoors, keep the back 20cm (8in) of the box free to plant out your seedlings later.
3. Leave a space of 15cm (6in) from the lupins and sow the cornflower seeds.
4. Leave another space of 15cm (6in) and sow the poppy in the front.
5. Cover the seeds with a thin layer of soil and carefully press it level.
6. Mist with water from a spray bottle so that the seeds remain in place.
7. If necessary, stick plant labels in the soil.

You can also mix the seeds of the cornflower and poppy to make your box look nice and wild. Just like a bouquet in a vase.

WHAT YOU NEED

+ A READY-TO-USE BOX
  (40cm/16in deep) with 5cm (2in)
  hydro grains and 5cm (2in) potting
  compost (soil)
+ EXTRA POTTING COMPOST (SOIL)
+ LUPIN SEEDS (make sure to choose
  seeds from an annual variety, such
  as the Lupinus perennis)
+ CORNFLOWER SEEDS
  (Centaurea cyanus)
+ POPPY SEEDS
  (Papaver somniferum)

FLOWERS

+ LUPIN (Lupinus perennis)

Sow the pea-like lupin seeds directly in the
ground from April to July. They germinate
quickly and flower the same year. Pick
lupins when the bottom flowers have just
opened. The rest will open in the vase.
After flowering, cut the lupins to just above
the ground. If you leave the roots, the
plants will grow the following year and
flower in early spring.

+ CORNFLOWER (Centaurea cyanus)

Sow cornflower seeds from late March to
early May directly in the ground. Within 2–3
weeks you will see the first shoots appear.
One plant gets about 20 flowers, so make

FLOWER FACT

Somnius is the Latin for sleep. The
Latin name *papaver somniferum*
stems from the fact that the sap
from the plant is poisonous in large
quantities, leading to a slow death.

sure they are about 20cm (8in) apart.
Cornflower seeds lose their germinative
power within a few years, so pay close
attention to the best before date.

+ POPPY (Papaver somniferum)

Sow from March to May for flowering in
the same year, or in August and September
for flowering the following year. To enjoy
flowers for longer, sow the poppy 2 or 3
times with intervals of a few weeks. Sear
the stems (see page 116) to enjoy the cut
flowers at their best. Leave the poppies
after flowering to produce seed pods that
look good in dried bouquets.

CARE

The cornflower produces more buds if you
remove the dead flowers. Other than that,
the varieties in this box require little care.
Ensure that the soil does not dry out.

FRESH AND DRIED

STRAWFLOWER, WINGED EVERLASTING AND LOVE-IN-A-MIST ARE GOOD AS CUT FLOWERS IN YOUR GARDEN BOUQUET, BUT THEY ARE ALSO VERY SUITABLE FOR DRIED BOUQUETS AND WREATHES.

☀ **Position:** sun

❀ **Sow:** in April, all varieties can be planted direction directly into the box at the same time

❀ **Flowering time:** June–October

1. Winged-Everlasting **2.** Strawflower **3.** Love-in-a-mist

WHAT YOU NEED

+ A READY-TO-USE BOX *(40cm/16in deep)* *with 5cm (2in) hydro grains and* *5cm (2in) potting compost (soil)*
+ EXTRA POTTING COMPOST (SOIL)
+ STRAWFLOWER SEEDS *(Helichrysum bracteatum)*
+ WINGED EVERLASTING SEEDS *(Xeranthemum annuum)*
+ LOVE-IN-A-MIST SEEDS *(Nigella damascena)*

FLOWERS

✦ LOVE-IN-A-MIST
(Nigella damascena)

How did this elegant bloomer get its quirky name? Perhaps due to the fact that the graceful flower is surrounded by a veil of thin, feathery leaves. You can easily extract seeds from the seed pods that emerge after flowering to enjoy your love-in-a-mist again the following year.

✦ WINGED EVERLASTING
(Xeranthemum annuum)

The seeds of the winged everlasting germinate quickly; after about 10–15 days you will probably see shoots appearing above the ground. The flowers are white or pink and are papery to the touch, hence their name 'everlasting'. In fact, they are already as good as dry when they flower, so making a dried bouquet couldn't be easier!

✦ STRAWFLOWER SEEDS
(Helichrysum bracteatum)

The predominant colours of the strawflower are: yellow, orange, red, pink and white. Pick them – if you want to dry them – when they're half open, then hang them upside down in a well-ventilated area. They will open completely, and in dried form they retain a strikingly beautiful

TIP

The seeds of love-in-a-mist can also be used as a spice in the kitchen, known as kalonji or black cumin. When you nibble on them, they taste a bit like spicy oregano. In Indian cuisine, black cumin is widely used in vegetable dishes, or as a seasoning on naan bread.

colour. Leave the hardy strawflowers in place after flowering to self-seed, so you can enjoy them again the following year.

CARE

Thin the seedlings a little if they have grown too close together. Other than that, you don't have to worry about the varieties in this box. If you want to use the strawflower and winged everlasting as a dried flower, it is best to pick them in full bloom. Love-in-a-mist, on the other hand, should be left until after flowering, when it forms decorative seed pods. There is a good chance that the strawflower and love-in-a-mist will self-seed and come up again the following year without you having to do anything.

GETTING STARTED

1. Fill the box to about 20cm (8in) below the edge with potting compost.

2. Sow the strawflowers in the back of your box, as these will grow the tallest. Leave a space of at least 5cm (2in) from the edge of the box.

3. Leave a space of 15cm (6in) from the strawflowers and sow the love-in-a-mist.

4. Leave another space of 15cm (6in) from the strawflowers and sow the winged everlasting.

5. Mist with water from a spray bottle.

6. If necessary, stick plant labels in the soil.

For these varieties, it also works really well if you mix the seeds and scatter them over the box. Then a pretty mix of blooms will appear.

LITTLE SWEETHEART SWEET PEA

THESE BUTTERFLY-LIKE FLOWERS IN CANDY FLOSS HUES LOOK LOVELY IN SMALL VASES, WHERE THE BLOOMS AND SCENT WILL LAST FOR A LONG TIME. THIS PLANT LOVES TO CLIMB, SO CONSTRUCT A SUPPORT IN THE BOX.

☀ **Position:** sun

❀ **Sow:** in April, directly in the ground. Pre-sowing can be done in February in a cool place where it is at least 5°C (41°F), but not too hot, such as a spare room. Use pots of at least 15cm (6in) deep, as the sweet pea grows a long taproot. You can plant the plants outside from late April.

❀ **Flowering time:** June–September

BIOLOGISCHE POTGROND

15CM (6IN)

GETTING STARTED

1. First, soak the sweet pea seeds in a bowl of water for 24 hours.

2. Fill the box to about 15cm (6in) below the edge with potting compost.

3. Make wigwam shapes with the bamboo canes by tying them together at the top.

4. Use your finger to make 2 holes about 2cm (¾in) deep next to each cane and place the sweet pea seeds in these holes. Have you pre-sowed? Then plant 2 or 3 plants next to each cane.

5. Cover the seeds with a thin layer of soil and carefully press it level.

6. Mist with water from a spray bottle so that the seeds do not move.

7. If necessary, stick plant labels in the soil.

WHAT YOU NEED

+ A READY-TO-USE BOX *(40cm/16in deep)*
  with 5cm (2in) hydro grains and
  5cm (2in) potting compost (soil)
+ EXTRA POTTING COMPOST (SOIL)
+ SWEET PEA SEEDS *(such as* Lathyrus
  odoratus *'Cupid', a dwarf variety of max.*
  40cm/16in height)
+ BAMBOO CANES
+ TWINE

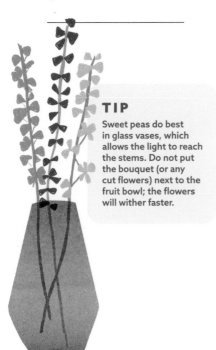

TIP
Sweet peas do best
in glass vases, which
allows the light to reach
the stems. Do not put
the bouquet (or any
cut flowers) next to the
fruit bowl; the flowers
will wither faster.

FLOWERS

+ SWEET PEA *(Lathyrus odoratus)*

The sweet pea looks super sweet, but
does have its demands: a well-fertilized
soil and sufficient drinking water for
optimal flowering.

CARE

Check regularly during growth that the
plants can find the canes to climb up,
regularly tying them to the cane to help
the shoots to grow straighter. When the
seedlings emerge, you can top (shorten)
the plant after the second pair of leaves,
which will encourage extra side shoots,
creating a fuller plant that can produce
more flowers.

If you want to grow sweet peas again
next year, you will need to use another
box, or replace the soil as soil fungus
may develop, causing the plant to die.

Note: birds and mice love sweet pea
seeds. Put your box in a sheltered place
to prevent your seeds from being eaten.

WILD AND WAVING GRASS

COSMOS IS A COLOURFUL EYE-CATCHER THAT SOMETIMES FLOWERS UNTIL NOVEMBER. ALONG WITH WAVING SWITCHGRASS – ANOTHER TALL PLANT – YOU GET A FULL, QUITE WILD BOX FROM WHICH YOU CAN CUT FLOWERS FROM FOR A LONG TIME.

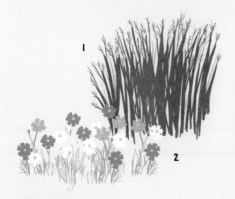

1

2

WHAT YOU NEED

+ A READY-TO-USE BOX *(40cm/16in deep) with 5cm (2in) of hydro grains and 5cm (2in) potting compost (soil)*
+ EXTRA POTTING COMPOST (SOIL)
+ COSMOS SEEDS *(Cosmos bipinnatus)*
+ SWITCHGRASS SEEDS *(Panicum virgatum)*

☀ **Position:** sun

❀ **Sow:** in April, directly in the ground

✿ **Flowering time:** June–October

1. Switchgrass **2.** Cosmos

FLOWERS

+ COSMOS *(Cosmos bipinnatus)*

With cosmos you have guaranteed success. It is a large, easy plant that flowers abundantly and for a very long time. In addition to humans, bees and butterflies are also happy with this garden favourite. Pick cosmos when the buds have burst open, but are not yet in full bloom, and they will stay fresh for longer in a vase. The flowers have fine, delicate leaves, so be gentle when handling. In August, sprinkle some organic fertilizer pellets at the base of the cosmos to make it grow and bloom even more.

+ SWITCHGRASS *(Panicum virgatum)*

Switchgrass is a particularly decorative ornamental grass that flowers in late summer and autumn with airy, golden brown plumes. This strong plant thrives best in full sun. The colours of both the leaves and the flower panicles change from golden brown to yellow ochre in the autumn, which is a feast for the eyes.

CARE

Cosmos can grow crooked after a while. Add a bamboo cane for support, and tie the stem to it. It is an annual variety that you remove from the box after the flowering season. If the switchgrass has rooted well, it will survive the winter and you can leave it in the box. In March, cut the grass back to 20cm (8in) above the ground, and it will sprout fresh growth in the spring.

SEED COLLECTION

Harvesting seeds from cosmos is very easy. After flowering, tufts with black 'sticks' remain; these are the seeds. Collect them and leave them for a few days to dry on newspaper. Then they will remain capable of germinating for about 4 years if you store them in an envelope in a cool, dry and dark place.

GETTING STARTED

1. Mix the cosmos and switchgrass seeds together.

2. Fill the box to about 20cm (8in) below the edge with potting compost.

3. Sprinkle the seed mixture over your box and press lightly.

4. Water thoroughly with a spray bottle.

5. If necessary, stick plant labels in the soil, stating which varieties you have sown in this box.

✺ **MAY** ❋ **JUNE–OCTOBER (FOLLOWING YEAR)**

BEE AND BUTTERFLY BUDDIES

THESE UNIQUELY SHAPED FLOWERS ARE GUARANTEED TO ATTRACT BEES AND BUTTERFLIES INTO THIS BOX – THEY ARE BRIMMING WITH NECTAR AND POLLEN. *NOTE:* THEY ARE BIENNIALS, SO THEY FLOWER A YEAR AFTER YOU HAVE SOWN THEM. IF YOU WANT TO SEE FLOWERS EARLIER, BUY FULLY GROWN PLANTS FROM AN ORGANIC SUPPLIER.

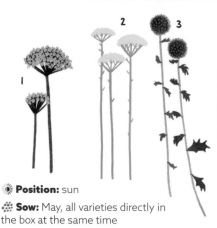

☀ **Position:** sun

✺ **Sow:** May, all varieties directly in the box at the same time

❋ **Flowering time:** June–October the following year

1. Verbena **2.** Yarrow **3.** Globe Thistle

WHAT YOU NEED

+ A READY-TO-USE BOX *(40cm/16in deep)* with 5cm (2in) hydro grains and 5cm (2in) potting compost (soil)
+ EXTRA POTTING COMPOST (SOIL)
+ VERBENA SEEDS *(Verbena bonariensis)*
+ YARROW SEEDS *(Achillea filipendulina 'Cloth of Gold')*
+ GLOBE THISTLE SEEDS *(Echinops ritro)*

- 70 -
PLANTING SCHEMES

GETTING STARTED

1. Fill the box to about 20cm (8in) below the edge with potting compost.

2. Sow the verbena in the back of your box, as this plant will grow the tallest. Leave a space of at least 5cm (2in) from the edge of the box.

3. Leave a space of 15cm (6in) from the verbena and sow the yarrow.

4. Leave another space of 15cm (6in) from the yarrow and sow the globe thistle.

5. Mist with water from a spray bottle.

6. If necessary, stick plant labels in the soil, stating which varieties you have sown in this box.

FLOWERS

◆ VERBENA *(Verbena bonariensis)*

Verbena is a tall-stemmed plant that can grow up to 1.5m (5ft) tall, with small purple flower clusters at the top. The plant continues to branch, which gives a playful effect, and it 'weaves' plants together. For this reason it is also called a weaving plant. You will soon spot that butterflies and bees are wild about it. Keep in mind that after the first year it will reappear everywhere, because it multiplies easily.

◆ YARROW *(Achillea filipendulina 'Cloth of Gold')*

The beautiful yellow umbellifers of the yarrow flowers are also very popular with bees and butterflies. The fern-like leaves of the plant give off an aromatic fragrance. And, if there is one flower suitable for drying, it is yarrow as, in contrast to many other bloomers, it retains its deep colour when dried.

◆ GLOBE THISTLE *(Echinops ritro)*

The Ancient Greek name 'echinops' means hedgehog. One look at this plant and you immediately understand where the name comes from. The small blue flowers grow together and form a spherical, spiky globe, that is very suitable as a dried flower. The globe thistle plant does not like to be moved, so it is preferable to sow it directly in the desired location. After the first bloom in August, cut it back to the base – with a bit of luck it will grow again for a second bloom in September and October.

CARE

Sowing verbena requires extra patience; germination can be irregular and spread over a longer period of time. The plant is readily available from nurseries, so you can also buy plants to make it easy on yourself. After germination, the seedlings can grow too close together; carefully remove a plant here and there. Verbena will simply remain green in a mild winter. Do not prune it back to the base of the plant until March of the following year.

FLOWER FACT

Verbena is attributed with numerous medicinal properties: the fast healing of wounds, lowering of high blood pressure, an analgesic for rheumatism and nerve pain, and a panacea for coughs and fever. It is a remedy for almost all ailments!

CREATING A WILDLIFE GARDEN

IT'S TIME TO TURN OUR ATTENTION TO HOW YOUR BOXES CAN NOT ONLY LOOK GOOD, BUT ALSO DO GOOD. BIODIVERSITY IS AT RISK THROUGH THE EXCESSIVE USE OF PESTICIDES, MAKING IT HARDER FOR POLLINATORS, SUCH AS BEES AND BUTTERFLIES, TO FIND FOOD WHICH IS PUTTING THEM IN DANGER OF EXTINCTION. USE YOUR BOXES TO MAKE THEM HAPPY AGAIN.

Without bees – which pollinate plants – the entire food chain collapses. However, there is a tiny ray of hope: your box flower garden can provide food and shelter in urban spaces where garden design trends have created more decks and patios, and fewer plants. You will notice that bees go wild for small scabious, dahlia, verbena, autumn aster, agastache, echinacea, monkshood, gypsophila, globe thistle, allium and lupins. In addition, there are various seed mixes available that are also very popular for attracting pollinators. In this small way you can contribute to and expand the biodiversity in your city.

BUTTERFLY PARADISE

Plants such as verbena, small scabious, globe thistle, echinacea and Japanese anemone are perfect for luring butterflies into your garden as they contain extra nectar, a superfood packed with nutritious sugars, proteins and vitamins. In addition, butterflies recharge themselves in the sun, and look for quiet places to sunbathe where it isn't draughty or windy. Create such a resting place by planting a few nectar-rich plants in a calm location. Perennial honesty, ox-eye daisy, allium and autumn aster are also suitable varieties.

There is plenty of choice to turn your cut flower garden into a true butterfly paradise. So, lay out the red carpet for cabbage whites, red admirals, peacock butterflies and little foxes.

TIP

Scatter bee seed mix in your guerilla garden or around the base of trees in the street.

BEE HOTEL

Do you want to do something extra for butterflies and bees? Then hang a butterfly house or bee hotel where they can shelter and nest – put some twigs and leaves in it to make it extra cozy for them. Butterflies will not camp there permanently, but they will hide from the rain or take a nap. On the other hand, wild bees do settle in a bee hotel. They lay eggs in the tubes or corridors, and brick the corridors from the inside to protect their larvae. As soon as it becomes warmer outside, the small bees leave their cocoon in search of flowers to enjoy their nectar. Don't be afraid that they will be a nuisance; bees only sting when they feel threatened.

BEES LOVE ...

+ autumn aster (1)
+ gypsophila (2)
+ verbena (3)
+ lupin (4)
+ globe thistle (5)
+ dahlias (6)
+ echinacea (7)
+ small scabious (8)
+ agastache (9)
+ monkshood (10)
+ allium

There are also various special seed mixes that you can buy with varieties that attract bees and butterflies. Plant your boxes with these varieties and create a wildlife haven that makes everyone's environment greener.

ECHINACEA AND SUNFLOWERS

THE SUNFLOWER – THE SYMBOL OF SUMMER – TURNS ITS FACE TOWARDS THE WARM SUN. ECHINACEA, WHICH ORIGINATES FROM THE SAME PLANT FAMILY, CONTINUES TO FLOWER WELL INTO AUTUMN, AND IS BEST KNOWN FOR ITS MEDICINAL POWERS.

☀ **Position:** sun

❀ **Sow:** sunflower can be pre-sown indoors from early March, or directly in the soil outside from mid-April. Growing echinacea seeds is not that easy so buying a plant is recommended and you instantly have beautiful blooming flowers!

✿ **Flowering time:** June–October

1. Echinacea **2.** Sunflower

WHAT YOU NEED

* A READY-TO-USE BOX *(40cm/16in deep) with 5cm (2in) hydro grains and 5cm (2in) potting compost (soil)*
* EXTRA POTTING COMPOST (SOIL)
* SUNFLOWER SEEDS *(Helianthus annuus 'Sunspot')*
* TWO ECHINACEA PLANTS *(Echinacea purpurea)*

FLOWERS

* SUNFLOWER
  (Helianthus annuus 'Sunspot')

There are countless sunflower varieties, with the main difference being the height; they can vary from 40cm (16in) to as much as 450cm (16in to 15ft)! So, choose a type that matches the layout of your boxes in terms of height. *Helianthus annuus* 'Sunspot' is a relatively low variety, reaching about 60cm (24in) tall. The flower may need some support, so carefully tie it to a bamboo cane. Do not do this too tightly, as you may pinch the stem so the plant can no longer absorb moisture. For use in bouquets, cut the sunflower stem diagonally when the flower is almost completely open. Then the blooms will stay fresh for longer in a vase.

* ECHINACEA *(Echinacea purpurea)*

Echinacea, or coneflower, has a large, conical-shaped flower heart and dark pink petals that hang slightly. Unlike most cut flower varieties, you do not have to dead head echinacea, because the flower heads also look attractive at this stage. Echinacea is a perennial that can simply remain in your box. Do not prune it until March, so that you can enjoy it even when it has finished flowering. If the temperature drops to below freezing for long periods in the winter, cover it with a good layer of leaves to protect the plant.

CARE

Both varieties like nutritious soil, so sprinkle some compost around the plants halfway through the season. It is important that the soil is always slightly moist – give extra water, especially in extreme heat in the summer. After flowering, you can leave the sunflowers in place to let the seeds ripen, and echinacea still looks decorative long after it has reached its peak.

GETTING STARTED

1. Fill the prepared box to about 20cm (8in) below the edge with potting compost.

2. Mentally divide your box in half and sow the sunflowers on one side, or plant your seedlings there if you have pre-sown indoors. Leave a space of about 15cm (6in) between the plants.

3. Plant the echinacea plants on the other side of your box, if necessary fill the remaining space with potting compost, and press down firmly.

4. Finally, water well so that the plants can take root in their new location.

BOX FULL OF DAHLIAS

BECAUSE THE DAHLIA IS A POPULAR CUT FLOWER VARIETY AND NEEDS A LOT OF SPACE, IT GETS ITS OWN BOX. THERE ARE A DIZZYING NUMBER OF DAHLIA VARIETIES – MORE THAN 200,000! FOR YOUR BOX, CHOOSE THE SOMEWHAT SHORTER VARIANTS, FOR EXAMPLE: 'MARBLE BALL', 'PINK MAGIC' OR 'ARABIAN NIGHT', AND MIX THEM UP.

☀ **Position:** sun

🌢 **Plant:** plant dahlia tubers after the last night frost, from approximately late April

✽ **Flowering time:** from mid-July to the first night frost

WHAT YOU NEED

+ A READY-TO-USE BOX *(40cm/16in deep)* with 5cm *(2in)* hydro grains and 5cm *(2in)* potting compost *(soil)*
+ EXTRA POTTING COMPOST (SOIL)
+ 4 DAHLIA TUBERS *different varieties*

15CM
(6IN)

GETTING STARTED

1. Fill the box to about 15cm (6in) below the edge with potting compost.
2. Place the tubers in the potting compost with the 'flat' side up, because that's where the shoots emerge.
3. Cover the tubers with a maximum of 5cm (2in) of soil and press gently.
4. Finally, give plenty of water.

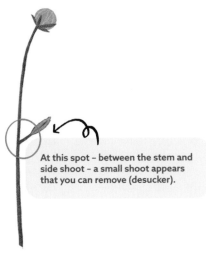

At this spot – between the stem and side shoot – a small shoot appears that you can remove (desucker).

FLOWERS

+ DAHLIA *(Dahlia)*

Cutting flowers stimulates the production of new buds, which is why you do not have to hold back with the dahlia. A good time is when the flower is about three-quarters open, but if you find dry or sticky petals at the back, it has already had its day. In the case of sturdy, freshly coloured petals, you can be sure that the dahlias will remain beautiful in a vase for about a week.

CARE

Warning! Dahlia shoots are loved by snails. So, keep a close eye on your box as soon as the plants are above the soil. Halfway through flowering, around August, you can sprinkle some organic fertilizer at the base. This ensures strong plants. When you see the flowers leaning, tie the stems loosely to a cane. If you would like long stems and large flowers, you can desucker the plants: remove the side shoots from the axil of the plant, where a sucker grows between the main stem and a side shoot (see left).

Dahlia tubers are not hardy, so you need to remove them from the soil at the first night frost. But first cut the plants back to about 15cm (6in) above the soil. Turn the plants upside down so that any water can drain from the hollow stems. This prevents them from rotting due to being too wet. Keep the tubers in a dark, cool and draught-free place, preferably covered. You can do this with a natural material such as peat dust, but also with a few old newspapers. Packing in clingfilm (plastic wrap) is also an option. However, make sure that there is no more soil on the tubers. In the spring, bring the tubers out again, they can be planted in the outside in May.

TIP

Ideally, cut dahlias in the morning or evening and put them in a good amount of water so they will last longer.

PARTIAL SHADE BOXES

EVEN IF YOUR BALCONY IS NOT IN THE SUN ALL DAY, THERE ARE PLENTY OF COLOURFUL BOXES TO CHOOSE FROM. FOR EXAMPLE, GO FOR BEAUTIFUL BULBS OR COTTAGE GARDEN CLASSICS SUCH AS FOXGLOVES. IT'S EVEN WORTH TRYING A FEW SUN WORSHIPPERS IN PARTIAL SHADE – THEY MAY DO BETTER THAN YOU THINK.

BEAUTIFUL BULBS

WE ARE ALL FAMILIAR WITH THE TULIP BUT IT'S WORTH LOOKING OUT FOR SPECIAL VARIETIES, SUCH AS THE SERRATED 'BLACK PARROT'. ITS INTENSE COLOUR MAKES A BEAUTIFUL COMBINATION WITH THE ROUND-HEADED ALLIUM AND THE CUTE BELLS OF LILY-OF-THE-VALLEY. THEY ALSO FLOWER EARLY AND FOR A LONG TIME!

WHAT YOU NEED

+ A READY-TO-USE BOX *(40cm/16in deep)* with 5cm *(2in)* hydro grains and 5cm *(2in)* potting compost *(soil)*
+ EXTRA POTTING COMPOST (SOIL)
+ LILY-OF-THE-VALLEY BULBS *(Convallaria majalis)*
+ 10 ALLIUM BULBS *(Allium 'Red Mohican')*
+ 10 TULIP BULBS *(Tulipa 'Black Parrot')*

☀ **Position:** partial shade
● **Plant:** late September–November
❋ **Flowering time:** April–August
1. Tulip **2.** Alium **3.** Lily-Of-The-Valley

FLOWERS

◆ LILY-OF-THE-VALLEY
  (Convallaria majalis)

The lily-of-the-valley is not really known as a suitable cutting flower, but if you put its stems with their cute dangling bells in a small vase, you will have a lovely bouquet. The lilies do not need much care; just make sure that the soil remains slightly moist and let the leaves die off naturally after flowering.

Note: lily-of-the-valley is poisonous. So don't eat it, but you probably didn't intend to do that anyway!

◆ ALLIUM *(Allium 'Red Mohican')*

Also known as the ornamental onion, alliums are available in all kinds of varieties. We chose a variety for this box that is slightly unusual: the 'Red Mohican'. Its beautiful deep red colour and considerable height provide a special accent in the box. If the stem is bent, don't worry, because just before flowering it will extend itself completely. If you bruise the leaf or stem, an onion scent will be released, but fortunately it will disappear as soon as you put it in water. Alliums also do well as dried flowers.

◆ TULIP *(Tulipa 'Black Parrot')*

The black parrot tulip is deep purple (almost black), shiny on the outside and matt on the inside. The leaves have frayed edges, which gives a playful effect. The beautiful long stems make this tulip very suitable as a cut flower.

CARE

The bulbs in this box do not require much care. Both lily-of-the-valley and allium are perennial and self-propagating, so you can leave them in the box after flowering. The perennial black parrot tulip generally does best in the first year, so you might want to remove it from the box after the flowering period.

FLOWER FACT

On May 1st, Labour Day in Northern France and Southern Belgium, it is customary to give each other a bunch of lily-of-the-valley as a symbol of happiness.

GETTING STARTED

1. For the first layer, plant the allium bulbs, tip up on the base layer of potting compost. Make sure the bulbs are close together but not touching.

2. Cover the allium bulbs with a layer of soil at least 5cm (2in) deep.

3. Now plant the second layer with tulip bulbs. Give them a bit more space than the bulbs in the bottom layer.

4. Cover again with at least 5cm (2in) of soil.

5. Plant the third layer with lily-of-the-valley bulbs.

6. Cover the top layer of bulbs with a layer of soil and press lightly.

7. Water the bulbs a little and place the box in a spot in partial shade.

COTTAGE GARDEN BOX

THE VARIETIES IN THIS BOX NEED A SEASON TO GROW INTO STRONG PLANTS AND WILL ONLY FLOWER IN THE SECOND YEAR; THE WAIT IS WORTH IT FOR A LOVELY DISPLAY! IF YOU'RE TOO IMPATIENT THEN YOU CAN BUY THE PLANTS INSTEAD FROM AN ORGANIC NURSERY FOR INSTANT IMPACT.

☀ **Position:** partial shade

⁘ **Sow/Plant:** foxglove can be pre-sown from June to August and planted in September/October. It is also possible to sow directly outside in August. You can sow monokshood in October directly outside. Sow Perennial Honestly in June or July and plant them in October where you want them.

❀ **Flowering time:** April–October of the following year

1. Tulip **2.** Monkshood
3. Perennial Honesty

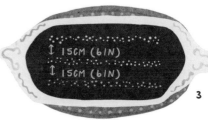

GETTING STARTED

1. Fill the box to about 20cm (8in) below the edge with potting compost.

2. Plant the foxglove in the back of your box, as this will grow the tallest. Leave a space of at least 5cm (2in) from the edge of the box.

3. Leave a space of 15cm (6in) from the foxglove and sow the monkshood.

4. Leave a space of 15cm (6in) from the monkshood and sow or plant the perennial honesty.

5. Fill any holes with soil where necessary and finally water thoroughly with a spray bottle.

6. If necessary, stick plant labels in the soil, stating which varieties you have sown in this box.

WHAT YOU NEED

+ A READY-TO-USE BOX *(40cm/16in deep)*
  with 5cm (2in) of hydro grains and 5cm
  (2in) potting compost (soil)
+ EXTRA POTTING COMPOST (SOIL)
+ MONKSHOOD SEEDS *(Aconitum*
  napellus)
+ FOXGLOVE SEEDS *(Digitalis purpurea)*
+ PERENNIAL HONESTY SEEDS *(Lunaria*
  rediviva)

FLOWERS

+ MONKSHOOD *(Aconitum napellus)*
Sow monkshood in September or
October in your box for early flowering
from June the following year. You can also
sow in March and April; then plant the
seedlings in October where you want
them to flower the following year. After
flowering, cut the dead stems to just
above the soil. The plant is hardy so will
reach maturity again next year. The
monkshood has 5 bell-shaped flowers per
stem. The most common colour is deep
blue, but it can also be white, pale pink,
yellow and violet.

Note: monkshood is poisonous (both for
humans and pets). Wear gardening gloves
when working with this plant.

+ FOXGLOVE *(Digitalis purpurea)*
Pre-sow foxglove in June – this can be
done directly in your box. You can plant
the seedlings in September or October.
Thanks to its striking height, up to 90
flowers appear on one stem!

Note: foxglove sap is poisonous (for both
humans and pets) and can cause cardiac
arrhythmias. Wear gardening gloves.

+ PERENNIAL HONESTY *(Lunaria rediviva)*
Perennial honesty is known for its seed
pods, which look like tokens or coins. You
can dry the oval-shaped, transparent
membranes between which you can see
the seeds. In addition, perennial honesty
smells great at night.

CARE

Support foxglove stalks if it is very windy,
otherwise they are at risk of snapping. The
varieties in this box like nutritious soil, so
spread some compost over the soil mid
season. At the end of the season, prune
the monkshood so that it can grow again
in the spring. Leave the foxglove, then
there is a good chance that it will self-
seed. Perennial honesty is a strong plant
that does not require much care.

GREEN WINTER BOX

A BOX WITH PERENNIALS, SO THAT YOU CAN DISPLAY GREENERY THROUGH THE WINTER. YARROW, AGASTACHE AND QUAKING GRASS CONTINUE TO FLOWER YEAR AFTER YEAR, SO YOU CAN ENJOY THEM ENDLESSLY!

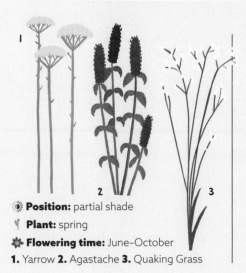

☀ **Position:** partial shade

🌱 **Plant:** spring

🌸 **Flowering time:** June–October

1. Yarrow **2.** Agastache **3.** Quaking Grass

WHAT YOU NEED

+ READY-TO-USE BOX *(40cm/16in deep) with 5cm (2in) hydro grains and 5cm (2in) potting compost (soil)*
+ EXTRA POTTING COMPOST (SOIL)
+ BAG OF HYDRO GRAINS
+ 1 YARROW PLANT *(Achillea filipendulina 'Cloth of Gold')*
+ 1 AGASTACHE PLANT *(Agastache rugosa 'Golden Jubilee')*
+ 1 QUAKING GRASS PLANT *(Briza media)*

FLOWERS

+ YARROW

(Achillea filipendulina 'Cloth of Gold')

The beautiful yellow umbellifers of the yarrow flowers are very popular with bees and butterflies. The fern-like leaves of the plant give off an aromatic fragrance. And, if there is one flower suitable for drying, it is yarrow as, in contrast to many other bloomers, it retains its deep colour when dried. Pick the yarrow when it is in full bloom, and hang the flowers upside down for a few weeks for best results.

+ AGASTACHE

(Agastache rugosa 'Golden Jubilee')

Agastache smells slightly of aniseed, and this bloomer is also very popular with bees and butterflies. The plant hates wet feet so limit the amount of water, and make sure that it does not catch too much rain in the autumn and winter. After flowering in March, cut the plant back to a few centimetres (an inch or so) above the soil, then it will flower again.

+ QUAKING GRASS *(Briza media)*

This ornamental grass waves in the wind, hence the name quaking grass. The spikes develop heart-shaped flowers that turn from white-yellow to violet-purple during

TIP

To make agastache tea, harvest the flowers in July and August, and allow them to dry completely then store in a sealed jar. Crush the flowers and use two teaspoons to brew a lovely sweet tea with a hint of licorice. Also good mixed with chamomile.

flowering. If it does not freeze too hard, the plant will remain beautifully green in the winter. Cut back in March to encourage new growth.

CARE

These perennial varieties are strong types that do not require much care. Water regularly in the first weeks after planting. For some extra nutrients, you can spread a layer of compost at the base of the plants. In the spring, remove the dead stems and leaves.

GETTING STARTED

1. Slightly loosen the roots at the bottom of the plants to encourage the growth of new, strong roots. Plant yarrow, agastache and quaking grass in your box.

2. Fill the gaps between the plants with soil and carefully press it down.

3. Finally, water well so that the plants can take root deeply in their new location.

CHEERFUL SHADE BLOOMERS

THIS BOX FULL OF CLASSICS - COLUMBINE, SMALL SCABIOUS AND GYPSOPHILA - FLOWERS FOR ALMOST THE WHOLE SEASON. THE PLANTS DO NOT NEED MUCH SUN, SO ARE IDEAL IF YOUR BALCONY, WINDOWSILL OR ROOF TERRACE IS SHADY.

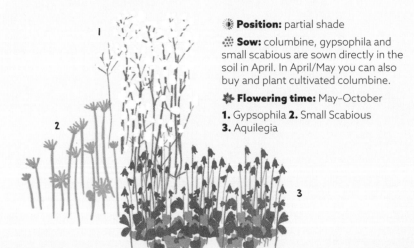

☀ **Position:** partial shade

✿ **Sow:** columbine, gypsophila and small scabious are sown directly in the soil in April. In April/May you can also buy and plant cultivated columbine.

❀ **Flowering time:** May–October

1. Gypsophila **2.** Small Scabious **3.** Aquilegia

WHAT YOU NEED

+ READY-TO-USE BOX *(40cm/16in deep)*
  with 5cm (2in) hydro grains and 5cm
  (2in) potting compost (soil)
+ EXTRA POTTING COMPOST (SOIL)
+ SMALL SCABIOUS SEEDS
  (Scabiosa atropurpurea)
+ GYPSOPHILA SEEDS
  (Gypsophila elegans)
+ COLUMBINE SEEDS OR PLANT
  (Aquilegia vulgaris)

FLOWERS

+ COLUMBINE *(Aquilegia vulgaris)*
Columbine is a strong plant that stands
out because of the deep blue-purple
colour of the flowers. As soon as the bell-
shaped flowers have finished flowering,
interesting-shaped seed pods appear with
which the plant also readily self-seeds. It
dies off on its own at the end of flowering,
but the roots survive, and this plant will
likely grow again the following year.

+ GYPSOPHILA *(Gypsophila elegans)*
Make sure the gypsophila plants are
ultimately about 20cm (8in) apart,
otherwise they will not have enough space
to grow. You can still dig out the plants and
move them until they are about 8cm (3in)
high. The springy flowers of gypsophila
give a playful touch to your cut flower
bouquet. Gypsophila also does well as a
dried flower. Pick the stems just before the
flowers open and hang them upside down
in bunches in a cool, dark place. After a
few weeks you will feel that the leaves
have become 'crispy' – a sign that they
have dried well.

FLOWER FACT

According to Floriography, the language
of flowers, small scabious is symbolic of
new love or the beginning of love; perfect
to give as a subtle hint when you have a
crush on someone.

◆ SMALL SCABIOUS
  (Scabiosa atropurpurea)

The great thing about small scabious is that you can enjoy it almost all summer long, as it flowers from June to September. With its purple-blue flowers on thin stems, this plant provides a special colour accent in your garden. Bees and butterflies are also thrilled by small scabious.

CARE

Columbine in particular loves humus-rich soil, so cover the soil with leaves and branches for example. The plant is hardy and has few other requirements. Gypsophila does not tolerate dried-out soil well. Therefore, keep an eye on the soil and water when the top layer feels dry. When the plant grows taller and more flowers start to bloom, that may cause the stems to become top heavy and droop a bit. In that case, tie them to a cane inserted into the soil next to the stem. If you cut the dead flowers of small scabious just above a leaf, you will encourage the production of new flowers.

GETTING STARTED

1. Fill the prepared box to about 20cm (8in) below the edge with potting compost.
2. Imagine the box divided into three.
3. Dig a hole on the left-hand side of your box to hold the columbine root ball and pour some water into it. Loosen the roots at the bottom of the plant a little with your fingers and put the columbine in the planting hole.
4. Sow the gypsophila seeds in the middle section.
5. Sow your small scabious in the right-hand section.
6. Cover the seeds with a thin layer of soil and carefully press level.
7. Mist the seedlings with water from a spray bottle.
8. If necessary, stick plant labels in the soil, stating which varieties you have sown in this box.

LATE BLOOMERS

WHEN THE SUMMER DISPLAYS ARE STARTING TO FADE, THIS BOX IS AT ITS ABSOLUTE BEST. YOU WILL ENJOY THE LONG-LASTING BLOOMS OF ASTER AND JAPANESE ANEMONE IN COMBINATION WITH GREAT MASTERWORT UNTIL WELL INTO THE AUTUMN .

☀ **Position:** partial shade

❄ **Sow/Plant:** bought plants are planted in the box in the autumn. You can also sow great masterwort in October/November but it will not flower until the following summer season. If you want flowers immediately, buy a plant of this variety.

✿ **Flowering time:** June–October

1. Autumn Aster **2.** Great Masterwort **3.** Japanese Anemone

WHAT YOU NEED

- 1 AUTUMN ASTER PLANT
  (Aster novae-angliae)
- 3 JAPANESE ANEMONE PLANTS
  (Anemone hupehensis)
- GREAT MASTERWORT SEEDS OR
  1 PLANT (Astrantia major)

FLOWERS

+ AUTUMN ASTER (Aster novae-angliae)
This is one of the most suitable aster
varieties for cut flowers because of its
long, sturdy stems. In bad weather and
in the evening, the pink-lilac flowers close.

+ JAPANESE ANEMONE
  (Anemone hupehensis)
The Japanese anemone comes in white,
pink or lilac. It is an easy plant that does
not make many demands on the soil.
The stems are hairy, and after flowering
the flowers form beautiful seed fluff;
do not prune the anemone immediately
after flowering!

+ GREAT MASTERWORT (Astrantia major)
A special bloomer with green-white
flowers, which also have a hint of pink in
them. This low-demand perennial does
well in any soil type. Great masterwort is
a suitable variety for drying. Pick the

flowers just before they are in full
bloom, then hang them upside down
for best results.

CARE

The varieties in this box are all perennials,
which you do not have to remove from the
box after flowering. If you cut back the
flower stems of great masterwort after the
first bloom, you have a good chance of
a second bloom in the autumn. The
Japanese anemone does not need to be
pruned; the autumn aster may be cut back
after flowering.

FLOWER FACT

Great masterwort has
its own Dutch name
(Zeeland button) due to
the fact that its beautiful
flower resembles the
traditional decoration
of the centuries-old
Zeeland costume.

GETTING STARTED

1. Plant the autumn aster and the Japanese anemone and, if not sowing seeds, the great masterwort in the box. In this case, skip steps 3 and 4.

2. Fill up the holes with soil until approximately 10cm (4in) below the edge of the box to create a level surface.

3. Sow the great masterwort seeds on the soil between the autumn aster and Japanese anemone.

4. Sprinkle another thin layer of soil over the whole area and press lightly.

5. Water in with a watering can.

◔ LATE SEPTEMBER–NOVEMBER ❋ JANUARY–MAY

WINTER COLOUR

PLANT THE DELICATE SPRING TONES OF SNAKE'S HEAD, DAFFODIL AND SNOWDROP IN THE AUTUMN, SO THAT IN JANUARY YOU CAN ENJOY THE FIRST FLOWERS IN YOUR BOX AND VASE. YOU CAN THEN REUSE THIS BOX FOR OTHER FLOWERS AFTER FLOWERING, PLANTING IT AGAIN IN SEPTEMBER WITH FRESH BULBS.

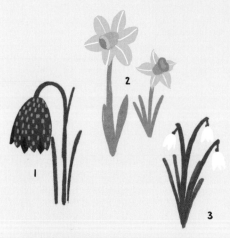

WHAT YOU NEED

+ A READY-TO-USE BOX *(40cm/16in deep)* *with 5cm (2in) of hydro grains and 5cm (2in) potting compost (soil)*
+ EXTRA POTTING COMPOST (SOIL)
+ 6 SNOWDROP BULBS *(Galanthus nivalis)*
+ 6 DAFFODIL BULBS *(Narcissus 'Yellow Cheerfulness')*
+ 6 SNAKE'S HEAD BULBS *(Fritillaria meleagris)*

☀/◑ **Position:** sun/partial shade

◔ **Sow/Plant:** late September–November

❋ **Flowering time:** January–May

1. Snake's Head **2.** Daffodil **3.** Snowdrop

GETTING STARTED

1. Plant the snake's head bulbs first in the prepared soil, with the tip facing up. Make sure the bulbs are close together but not touching.
2. Cover the snake's head bulbs with a layer of soil at least 5cm (2in) deep.
3. Plant the second layer with the daffodil bulbs. Give them a little more space between them than the bulbs below and make sure they do not touch each other.
4. Cover the second layer of bulbs with a layer of soil at least 5cm (2in) deep.
5. Plant the third layer with the snowdrop bulbs and cover this layer with some soil and press it lightly.
6. Water and put the box in a spot in the sun or partial shade.

FLOWERS

◆ SNOWDROP *(Galanthus nivalis)*
These are easy plants in themselves, but in the spring they do need plenty of light so make sure that they are not in the shade of other plants. You can propagate the bulbs after a year or two by digging up and dividing them at the end of the flowering time: break apart the bulbs that have grown together and replant the loose bulbs. The following year you can enjoy an extra avalanche of delicate white bells!

◆ DAFFODIL
   (Narcissus 'Yellow Cheerfulness')
This is a strong daffodil variety with a double flower, which gives off an intoxicating spring scent. Sometimes it has four flowers on one stem! The colour is a slightly softer yellow than usual and, as a result, it combines beautifully with the other varieties in the box.

FLOWER FACT
The snowdrop is the flower of hope and symbolizes 're-awakening and living intensely after a long winter'.

◆ SNAKE'S HEAD *(Fritillaria meleagris)*
A special flower because of the pattern that resembles the speckled shell of a lapwing egg. Just like snowdrops and daffodils, this bulbous plant likes moist soil. You can give it some extra compost as soon as it starts to grow, because this beauty likes to grow in nutritious soil.

CARE

The bulbs in this box are all hardy, so you can leave them in the soil after flowering. Thanks to the nutrition from the leaves, the bulbs will recharge for the next flowering season.

PART 3

CUTTING AND STYLING FLOWERS

A SEA OF FLOWERS IN YOUR HOME AS WELL AS ON YOUR BALCONY OR WINDOWSILL. IN THIS CHAPTER, YOU WILL FIND TIPS AND TRICKS FOR CUTTING AND STYLING YOUR FLOWERS AND KEEPING THEM BEAUTIFUL FOR AS LONG AS POSSIBLE IN A VASE.

FLOWER CUTTING TIPS

Take care when cutting flowers and follow these tips so your bunch will look fantastic in a vase for days.

TIMING

The best time to pick flowers is early in the morning or later in the evening. At these times, there is still a lot of moisture in the stems, so that they remain strong in the vase for longer. During the day – when the temperature rises – plants evaporate more water and the stem is weaker. If stems are broken or damaged when cutting, the moisture supply also decreases and in both cases, flowers will tend to droop more quickly in the vase.

SHARP SHEARS

Cut flowers diagonally with sharp pruning shears or a knife. Dull blades damage the stems and flowers will wilt more quickly.

CAREFUL PICKING

Cut flowers with care, so that no big gaps appear in your box. Make sure that you do not spoil the natural shape of the plant too much with your pruning shears.

LONG STEMS

Try to cut as many long stems as possible, so you can still vary your bouquet's height. By cutting the stem as deep as possible in the plant, the plant is also stimulated to grow new, long stems.

IN THE BUD

Make sure there are not too many closed buds in the stem that you cut. Usually they won't open when they are in the vase, while they will bloom on the plant. An exception to this are flowers in spikes, such as foxglove. Pick these when about half of the flowers are open. The rest will open in the vase, especially if you remove the lower dead flowers once in a while.

LONG DRINK

Immediately after cutting, place the flowers for a few hours in a clean bucket (pail) of water in the shade. Then they get the chance to absorb a lot of water, and they stay fresh for longer. If possible, keep short and long stems separate, so that the short flowers at the bottom of the bucket are not crushed.

ENJOY YOUR BOUQUET FOR AS LONG AS POSSIBLE

Your cut flowers will wilt if they are in the sun or near the heating, so make sure you display them in the coolest possible place. Clean water also helps to keep flowers fresh for longer. In polluted water, bacteria create a slimy substance that clogs the flower stems. Then they can no longer absorb water and the flowers quickly wilt. Change the water every two days.

CUT FLOWER FEED

You can add a dash of cut flower feed to the water in the vase. The feed consists of sugars that ensure that the flowers start and continue to bloom, and a bactericidal agent keeps the water in the vase clear for longer. You can also use a home-made remedy: mix a spoonful of sugar and a few drops of bleach.

CLEANING

Harmful bacteria can continue to grow in empty vases so clean your vases well after use before you put them away. Wash the vase with hot water and ecological detergent or bio soap.

STYLING FLOWERS

Now you can finally put your home-grown flowers in a vase! How do you make a lively bouquet with them and how will that bouquet stay fresh for a long time?

REMOVE LEAVES

First, strip off all the leaves from the stem that would otherwise be in the water. Leaves rot faster underwater, which can smell considerably. In addition, the flowers will wither faster due to the bacteria.

CUT DIAGONALLY

The xylem of plants (small vessels that can be compared to blood vessels) transports the water with the necessary nutrients to the leaves and flower. As soon as you cut off the flower, the bottom stem dries out and these vessels silt up. By removing a piece of the stem before you put the flowers in the vase, it can absorb water again. Use a clean and sharp knife and cut as diagonally as possible to create a larger area for the stem to absorb as much water as possible.

SEAR STEMS

Certain flower varieties, such as the poppy, can immediately droop when you put them in water. To prevent this, sear the lower part of the stems so that they can no longer lose their sap, which causes them to hang limp in the vase. Dip the stems in boiling water for 20 seconds and then immediately place them in a vase with lukewarm water. Make sure that the flowers do not come into contact with the steam from the hot water, because they will not survive.

FLOWER SHAPES

Flowers come in roughly three shapes that you can combine well with each other:

+ **Round**

  Flowers with a round shape include allium (1), dahlia (2), globe thistle and autumn aster (3). You can use them in your bouquet as an accent flower, because they attract attention.

+ **Pointed**

  Pointed or spike-shaped flowers point upwards on a single stalk. Examples include: agastache (4), foxglove (5), lupin (6) and ornamental grasses such as quaking grass and switchgrass.

+ **Branched**

  Flowers that have several florets on one flower head are called compound flowers. For example: gypsophila (9), verbena (8) and bishop's flower (7).

LIVELY

A bouquet is lively if it is not completely symmetrical. Let a striking flower or branch stick out, or allow a slanted stem to fall over the edge of the vase. An odd number of flowers also helps the arrangement to not look too 'perfect'. Work preferably with 3, 5 or 7 flowers, but don't stick to that too strictly. For example, use 3 large sunflowers, 5 medium flowers such as dahlias, and 9 or 11 fillers, such as

pot marigolds or ox-eye daisies. Then
you will soon have a lavish bunch that
still looks airy. Also, play with the length
of the stalks for visual variations.

Finally, turn the vase regularly while
arranging to check that the flower
arrangement looks beautiful on all sides.

EYECATCHER

Choose a few eyecatchers when compiling
your bunch. These can be the tallest stems
you have picked, but also striking flower
heads, such as dahlias, that stand out in
shape, colour or size.

FOLIAGE

Try making a bunch with a base
of foliage. Then choose different
leaf shapes and green colours to

create depth and variety. For example, eucalyptus has an attractive grey-green hue that combines beautifully with the deep green of asparagus. You can also add amaranthus and branches with berries for providing essential variety in shape and structure.

KEEPING UPRIGHT

If you put a few flowers upright in a vase, they will often lean or droop. To help, put some chicken wire in the vase and stick the stems through it, making sure the chicken wire isn't visible.

WHICH VASE?

The ratio of flowers to vase is in balance when the vase is one third to half the height of the tallest flowers and leaves. If the vase is taller, the flowers will appear only just over the edge, and with a vase that is too low, there is a risk that it will topple over when you put in the flowers.

SMALL VASES

Small vases are always appealing – you could also consider glass jars and milk bottles for variety. Make a mix of sizes, colours

and materials and for best results, use an odd number. Try groups of 3, 5, 7 or even 9 if you want to go large! You can put one or a few stems in the display and put a few eyecatching flowers in the spotlight. Or create a bouquet by placing several small vases together.

Flowers of the same shape, such as a pot marigold and ox-eye daisy, do not compliment each other so try to mix size and shape, for example combining a pointed flower such as agastache with a round bloom, such as dahlia. Add a branched flower like gypsophila and you're done! (See also page 120.)

THE SECRET OF A LOVELY BUNCH

FLOWERS IN A VASE ARE ALWAYS BEAUTIFUL, BUT HOW DO YOU MAKE A REALLY SPECIAL BOUQUET? LUCINDA VAN DER PLOEG, FLOWER STYLIST AT ONLINE FLORIST BLOOMON, REVEALS THE SECRET TO A BUNCH THAT HAS THE WOW FACTOR.

HARMONIOUS COLOUR PALETTE

The most important tip: create harmony. People often think of a colourful mix of flowers with a cut flower bouquet, but that quickly becomes a bit garish. That's why I think it's better to choose three main colours. Then I go for all kinds of shades within those colours. That way you have a playful bunch that is still in balance.

FIDDLY VERSUS CALM

Flowers have roughly three shapes: pointed, round and branched. It is good to vary the shapes. For example: a pointed gladiolus with a round gerbera or sunflower in combination with gypsophila, which falls into the category 'branched flowers'. If you were to only use these fiddly branched flowers, you would get a restless effect. By placing a large round flower on a bare stem, such as a gerbera or sunflower, you create a resting point, which is calming for the eyes.

EMOTIVE DESIGN

I mainly style a bouquet by feeling. Take a good look at the flowers, and find out what emotion they convey to you. Gladioluses, for example, are stimulating flowers because of their shape: long, straight stems that reach up to the sky. That image gives energy. But when you fill a vase with amaranthus, then you get a sad image. Amaranthus has a cascade movement: a sad posture. Just like a weeping willow, which is not called that for nothing. One amaranthus can be interesting for the composition of a bunch, but three amaranthuses are often too much of a good thing. Then sadness gets the upper hand. Whereas you probably want a bouquet to cheer you up, and perhaps also give you consolation.

INSTINCTIVE STYLE

When I look at a bunch that is not completely finished, as a flower stylist I immediately know what I am missing. Even as a layman you can develop that feeling. My standard advice is: take the time to put together a good bunch. First, sort all the flowers according to shape: pointed (gladiolus), round (rose or gerbera) and branched (gypsophila) together. Then put them in a vase. Don't begin with the largest flower, but the branched variety. This immediately creates volume and support for the rest of the flowers. Look carefully: do you think it is the right length in relation to the vase, or should you make it a bit shorter? Vary the lengths of your flowers and choose the right length for each flower. In this way, sufficient attention is paid to each individual flower. This is how you get started and eventually by practising you get a better sense of what fits well together.

OUT OF THE BOX

Try to think out of the box. If you put loose flowers in small vases, you may tend to make the stems much shorter. But it is much more exciting to leave them intact as much as possible. If you have a vase approximately 10cm (4in) tall, try stalks that are two or three times longer. You will get a surprising effect with such a composition.

THINK BIG

If you want to create a striking effect with three mini vases, place your vases at least 20cm (8in) apart and arrange your flowers with long stems, at least 2 or 3 times the height of your vases. This creates an exciting bouquet effect. You can play with your flowers and the vases in all kinds of ways.

STEP-BY-STEP FLOWER ARRANGING

STEP 1

Fill two-thirds of
a spotless vase
with lukewarm water.

STEP 2

Sort the stems according
to hard, soft and tall ones.

STEP 3

Cut 1cm (½in) off the stems
(again) diagonally, so that
the flower can absorb the
water well.

STEP 4

Remove all the leaves
that would otherwise be
below the rim of the vase.

STEP 5

First, take only the hard stems and put them one by one in the vase. Make sure that the flowers all point in opposite directions, so that the stems cross each other in the vase. By doing so, they form a sturdy framework.

STEP 6

Insert the soft stems into the frame you made with the hard stems, and keep turning the vase so that you can see from all sides whether the flowers look good in the vase.

STEP 7

Finally, put the tall stems in the vase. If done correctly, they should stay upright because they are held by the frame of the other stems.

STEP 8

View your bunch from all sides. Are there any gaps, does it look lively, are the colours well distributed? Check that all the stems are fully in the water. Satisfied? Enjoy your display of home-grown flowers!

DRYING FLOWERS

MEMORIES OF THAT ENDLESS FRENCH LAVENDER FIELD, AN UNFORGETTABLE SUMMER PICNIC IN A MEADOW SURROUNDED BY BUTTERCUPS, OR THE FIRST CORNFLOWERS FROM YOUR GARDEN, CAN BE SAVED BY DRYING FLOWERS. FURTHERMORE, DRIED FLOWERS ARE LONG-LASTING: ONCE THEY HAVE DRIED PROPERLY, THEY WILL REMAIN GOOD FOR YEARS.

AIR DRYING

The easiest method is air drying. This simply means that you tie the flowers together and hang them upside down in a cool, dry place. For this technique, it is useful to cut the flowers when they are not quite fully opened. Otherwise, they may lose their petals while drying. Remove the foliage from the bottom half of the stems beforehand as they dry less well, which slows down the process. Then tie the flowers together in bunches. Small flowers can be put in bunches of about 10 stems; large flowers can be hung separately. Do this in surroundings that are not too damp, otherwise there is a risk that the stalks will go mouldy with mildew. For best results, hang the bunches in a dark, ventilated room.

Depending on the type of flower, the drying process takes from one to a few weeks. Feel the leaves of the flowers to check whether they have dried completely. Are they a bit brittle? Then the job is done. You can also test this by placing the flowers in an empty vase. If the stems bend, it is better to leave them hanging a little longer. As an extra check, you can also keep the flowers in the light for a while. If they are translucent, then you're all good too.

FLOWER PRESS

Small, flatter flowers and foliage are easy to dry with pressure. This is possible with a flower press, but also works between two thick books. Always place the flowers between sheets of tissue paper, kitchen paper or newspaper to absorb the moisture that is pressed from the flowers. If you refresh the paper daily for the first few days, you will get the best results.

TIP

White flowers are less suitable for use in a press method because under pressure they turn brown quickly.

OVEN DRYING

It may sound strange at first, but you can also let your flowers dry in a convection oven. Flowers with many leaves and compact varieties such as roses, cornflowers and pot marigolds, are especially suitable for this method. You can randomly spread the flowers on the oven rack if you don't mind about the final shapes. Do you want to keep the original 'looks' intact as much as as possible? Then it is better to put chicken wire over the rack, and insert the stems with the flowers upwards. Then let them dry in the oven at 40°C (104°F) for a few hours. Exactly how long it takes depends on the quantity and the variety, so keep a close eye on everything! Use similar methods to air drying to check progress: drying is successful when the petals feel a little brittle or papery.

HERBARIUM

Flowers wilt, there is no way around that, but you can make tangible memories by drying your favourite flowers and storing them in a herbarium.

STEP-BY-STEP HERBARIUM

STEP 1

Collect the flowers you want to include in your herbarium. Pick and transport them with care.

STEP 2

Dry in a flower press or between a stack of heavy books. Change the paper every few days in the beginning to make drying faster and more effective.

STEP 3

When the plants are completely dried, you can then stick them in your herbarium. For example, choose a quality notebook with thick paper, so your flowers will stay attached. Make a pleasing composition of the flowers and stick the stems carefully with a piece of transparent tape. If you find it useful, you can write the variety and the year in which you grew the flower.

ABOUT THE AUTHOR

Jennita is the founder of The Plucking Studio. This studio was created out of her love for flowers and the desire to fill her life with them. It all started a few years ago in her garden, where she started growing fruit, vegetables and flowers with a friend. She soon found her passion for growing and decided to expand her garden into a small-scale flower nursery. It didn't take long for Jennita to realise that growing flowers sustainably was her favourite thing. The beauty, colours, shapes and scents of the flowers she nurtured from a seed never ceases to amaze her time and time again.

First published in 2020 by Snor
This English hardback edition published in 2021 by Quadrille

The rights to this book have been negotiated by Sea of Stories Literary Agency, www.seaofstories.com, Sidonie@seaofstories.com

First published in 2021 by Quadrille, an imprint of Hardie Grant Publishing
Quadrille
52–54 Southwark Street
London SE1 1UN
quadrille.com

TEXT Jennita Jansen
ILLUSTRATIONS Agnes Loonstra
DESIGN Esther Snel
FINAL EDITING Sarah-Mie Luyckx

THANKS TO Judith van Lent, Marjolein Lanfermeijer from *Plukjebloemen.nl* and Lucinda van der Ploeg from Bloomon

For the English language hardback edition:
PUBLISHING DIRECTOR Sarah Lavelle
SENIOR COMMISSIONING EDITOR Harriet Butt
JUNIOR DESIGNER Alicia House
HEAD OF PRODUCTION Stephen Lang
PRODUCTION CONTROLLER Sinead Hering

Text © Jennita Jansen 2021
Illustrations © Agnes Loonstra 2021
Design © Esther Snel 2021
and layout © Quadrille 2021

ISBN 978 1 78713 690 8
Printed in China

MIX
Paper from responsible sources
FSC™ C020056